Reminiscence, Reflections, and Recipes

Memories of Growing up in Hawaii

Marian M. Morey

Tutu's Woods Publishing

Reminiscence, Reflections, and Recipes: Memories of Growing up in Hawaii

Copyright 2021 © Marian M. Morey

Enlarged Print

Tutu Pa's Tales from the Taro Patch

Copyright 1982 © Conway Marcallino

All rights reserved. This book or any portion thereof may not be reproduced or used in any manner whatsoever without the express written permission of the publisher or author except for the use of brief quotations in a book review. Most photos in this book are under a limited license and may not be reproduced or sublicensed to a third party.

First Printing, 2021

ISBN-13: 978-1-7362993-2-6

Tutu's Woods Publishing

Raleigh, NC 27606

USA

Table of Contents

Introduction vi
Dedication vii
Chapter 1 1
Chapter 2 6
Chapter 3 12
Chapter 4 19
Chapter 5 25
Chapter 6 30
Chapter 7 35
Chapter 8 40
Chapter 9 47
Chapter 10 55
Recipes 66
    Seafood Bake 70
    Seafood Sauce 72
    Crab or Shrimp Dip 72
    Tartar Sauce and Tutu's Po' Boys 74
        Tartar Sauce 74
        Po' Boy 75
    Tutu's Dipping Sauce 77
    Pita Stuffers 77

Stuffed Flounder 78

Chinese Barbecue Roast Chicken or Pork 80

Chicken or Turkey Bake 81

Crab Cakes and Cocktail Sauce 84

    Crab Cakes 84

    Cocktail Sauce 86

Teriyaki 86

Tutu's Fried Rice 88

Slow Cooker Beef Soup with Onions 90

Italian Chicken Tortellini Soup 91

Swiss Steak 93

Japanese Stir Fry with Tofu 95

    Variation with Soba Noodles 97

Easy Tex-Mex Night at Tutu's 98

    Taco Beef 99

    Taco Chicken 99

    Nachos 100

    Quesadillas 100

    Tex-Mex Bacon Relish 101

    Easy Burrito Rollups 101

    Enchilada Bake 102

    Taco Casserole 102

Easy Chinese Spareribs 104

Sweet-and-Sour Barbecue Sauce 106

Streusel Love 108

    Fruit Streusel 109

    Quick Peach Streusel Cake 110

- Quick Orange Streusel Cake 110
- Blueberry Coffee Cake with Streusel and Cream Cheese Glaze 111
  - Cream Cheese Glaze 113
- Triple Fudge Brownies 113
  - Chocolate Cream Cheese Frosting 114
- French Cream 116
- Cream Pies 117
  - Banana Cream Pie 118
  - Pina Colada Cream Pie 118
  - Maple Pecan Pie 118
  - Chocolate Cream Pie 118
  - Coconut Cream Pie 119
- Trifle 120

Tutu Pa's Tales from the Taro Patch 122
- Da Ehu Kumu in Her Red Muumuu 122
- Da Nite Befoa Kalikamaka 127
- Keaka an da Lilikoi Vine 131
- Da Tree Leedle Peegs 135
- Da Tree Bares 140
- Da Kolohe Mo'o of da Wailuka Rivah 143
- Simple Simon's Pieman 147
- Peter Piper's Peppers, da Kine Pidgin 147
- Akeke Ella 148

Introduction

I started thinking of writing about my Hawaiian childhood because my experiences seem so different from those I hear about today. Many of the post-war years were lean years, with men coming home injured, finding jobs and making jobs in spite of their injuries. War widows found themselves working to support their children. Tourism was increasing and there was a growing awareness of the rest of the world. We made use of everything, wasted very little, and made as much as we could in the home. We shared everything we had and knew that if we didn't have something, our neighbor might have it. We were a mixed culture and it didn't matter. For the most part, we all got along, and were laid back about it.

Children could be children. We were sent out to play, and we did. We frequently made our own fun and didn't need to be entertained. Everyone had a job to do, even if it was only old Joe, telling stories and entertaining his great-grandsons. Our parents made their livings any way they could; children were expected to do their own work and chores, but also to play and learn. Learning was fun! We were encouraged to read and to be curious about everything. If you couldn't afford to buy a book, there was always the library! Tourism was a growing part of Hawaiian life back in the 1940s and '50s; many of my early jobs revolved around tourism and many of my friends were tourists who stayed.

All kids become the products of their upbringing and experiences, and in this book, I've tried to convey how it was for a typical girl, growing up in the middle of the Pacific Ocean. I am the sum of my forebears and experiences at a unique time in Hawaiian and American history. I am lucky to have lived during this time and in this place, and to this day, to provide my family and friends with the benefit of my experience.

Dedication

To my children and grandchildren.

i ka'u mau keiki a mo'opuna

To my new friends and old.

i ka'u mau hoaaloha hou a me kahiko

Aloha nui loa!

Honolulu cityscape

Chapter 1

Almost everyone has memories of their childhood, some that have faded, and some seem so clear. I always kept a diary in my youth and wrote my impressions down, so perhaps I do remember more than most people. Back in the 1940s when I was born, Hawaii was entirely different than it is today. If you travel to the outer islands today, you might find people living simply as they did back then, but tourism, modern life and the American military have made their marks in the modern day, especially on Oahu. Honolulu has gobbled up many of the pineapple and sugar cane fields and expanded to encompass much of Oahu south of the Ko'olau Mountains dividing city from rural and suburbia on the windward side. From the inside, Honolulu looks like most cities in the United States, but with low humidity, palm trees and a rich and unique history.

    Much of modern Honolulu would shock an old timer returning to the city today. In the 1940s and '50s, there were still old Victorian homes on the slopes of Punchbowl Crater, which holds National Memorial Cemetery of the Pacific. My first husband and my son who died too soon are in that cemetery, and I spent ten of my first twelve years there on Punchbowl's slopes. My great-grandparents had built and lived in the house, as did my parents and our family later. When I was twelve, my parents sold the property and moved us to Kaneohe to a more modern house on a mountain across the bay from the Marine Corps Air Station. My mother, particularly, being from the mainland, was tired of cleaning what she'd thought of as a relic. Decades later, visiting the property in a desire to experience a sense of "home" proved to be an eye opener and a shock to my system. The people who bought the property demolished everything and built a many-floored condominium on the spot. Everything that I had known and loved there was gone.

My sister Maile on the left, with me at our childhood home

My siblings and I loved living in that old Victorian. It was on a big plot of land with a caretaker's cottage, two huge dog kennels, a garden, clothes lines, rabbit hutches and chicken coops. We had two huge mango trees, banana trees, papaya trees, a fig tree, guava and lilikoi bushes. Along with the fruits and vegetables readily available, we had unlimited fresh fish, chicken, rabbit and pork from which to choose. We didn't raise pigs, but my dad always "knew someone." Besides the food we grew, we also had flower bushes and trees. Dad grew all sorts of orchids on the moss clinging to our big shade trees. We had several varieties of hibiscus in bright colors, plumeria trees (frangipani), pikakes, crown flowers, lehua and large ti leaf plants. It was always an adventure for us. We loved examining our folks' castoffs and furniture discarded in the attic. Our imaginations could run wild (along with us kids). Sometimes the mangoes would fall into the kennel closest to the house, and Michael, our terrier, loved and would eat them. They didn't seem to hurt him, and he liked mangoes the way some dogs like their bones. When he was down to the pit, he'd keep chomping away, and I remember my mother saying, "Darn, that dog will be teething forever!"

Those were the days before locking your doors. We played with other neighborhood kids who lived in houses similar to ours. We'd be outside from morning to dark, and even on school days, could run down to the beach at Waikiki with an adult. We had an old station wagon, and Dad loved to take us all to the beach. My dad had a big old-fashioned, koa wood surfboard, and once I could swim, he taught me how to surf. In those days, we'd have to wax the board for traction. When I was little, Dad would take me out on the board to the "good waves," wax the board, and give the board a push. Then I'd have to paddle like the devil to keep the momentum up. Once I was on the way, I could stand up all the way to the beach. I was six. I had to grow a bit before I was strong enough to paddle myself out to the best waves, but I'll never forget skimming over the cool water with the hot sun on my back. I usually had a piece of wax in my cheek, too, because I wanted to be like my dad.

We had the largest, juiciest tomatoes in Honolulu. Daddy was so proud of his tomatoes. He'd take trips down to the fish market and bring home fish entrails to incorporate into the soil at the base of his plants. My mother, though, was the disciplinarian, and her pride and joy was a little hot chili pepper bush outside our kitchen door. Like all kids, we practiced with swearing and trying to be cool and grown-up. Every time she heard us, however, we got hot chili pepper rubbed on our front teeth. (Even now, as an old lady, I only swear occasionally, I'm sure due to her influence—and still look around to see who's in the room.) I still use fish emulsion fertilizer, but nowadays it comes in bottles.

It works well enough that some of my houseplants are thirty and forty years old, and some are babies of those houseplants.

I give credit to Phylis who taught me how to make certain things in her kitchen, and she started when I was six or seven years old. Sometimes when I was a pain in the neck, hanging around and getting in the way, she'd turn to me and say, "Let's cook something!" I was short, and being so young, could hardly see over the top of her old gas range. It must have dated from the late 1920s or '30s. The very first thing she taught me was how to make seven-minute frosting on top of the stove. I knew the recipe back then, but I no longer do. I do remember standing on her husband's favorite chair with one of her aprons tied up under my arms, beating egg whites on top of the stove with the old-fashioned manual eggbeater. Phylis had a wealth of information and kitchen hints and told me I was a natural cook because I always knew what flavors went well together. She was an expert at tempura batters and Japanese cooking. And of course, she worked professionally as one of the cooks at Fisherman's Wharf.

Spence Weaver, Fisherman's Wharf. Credit Honolulu Star Advertiser. Thanks to Bob Sigall

For decades, Spence and Cliff Weaver, under the Spencecliff Corporation, owned many restaurants in Hawaii, the most notable being Fisherman's Wharf. My parents were friends with Cliff Weaver, and they spent many afternoons there. On weekends, my parents would take us in the old station wagon down to the Wharf or to Queen's Surf down at the far end of Waikiki. When we were at the Wharf, we kids would sit in the car and do our homework in front of the kitchen's big picture window. Phylis would wave to us and keep an eye on us, and she'd bring us inside to Cliff's office and to the bathroom for potty breaks. Every evening my parents partied in the restaurant, we kids would sit in Cliff's office with big slices of fresh fruit pie à la mode. Sometimes when the restaurant was busy because a ship had come from the mainland, she'd bring the goodies out to the car and leave Cliff's office door open for us.

My father loved Phylis's barbecue sauce, and he used to sprinkle hot chili pepper flakes on his barbecue sometimes. Phylis taught me how to make the sauce for our family, and I still make it today, although I'm a "throw" cook, and have changed it slightly over the years. I keep it by the quart or gallon in industrial-sized ketchup jars for the kids' and grandkids' visits, and it's always available for meats and seafoods that star in our cookouts. Living on the East Coast, with actual winters, half the year I'm oven-barbecuing, and this sauce works with most any cooked meat. It's great for pulled-meat barbecue sandwiches served on hot toasted buns as requested by the grandchildren or kids. I am their favorite short-order cook, hands down.

Chapter 2

I was born in Eleele, before World War II ended. My earliest memory is of my grandparent's home and their screened front porch. I remember wicker furniture and seats at a level with the top of my head. My very first words were "excuse me" when I tripped over a throw rug.

In those days, my grandparents were hands-on. We spent a lot of time with them, and we were happy to listen to tales of the old days. Grandma Mina had come from Hilo and had a rich and colorful heritage. Her grandmother was a descendant of the daughter of King Kalaniopu'u, Pualinui, first cousin to Kamehameha the Great, and was also a Pualinui. She married an Englishman, William Fredrick Conway, and they raised their daughters on the Big Island.

Great-Great Grandma Pualinui Kaheana Conway

Their daughter Emma married John H. Maby from the state of New York. They had a number of children, my Grandma Mina among them. Grandma grew up at the Volcano House, up on the rim of Kilauea Crater, and in Hilo. Her father was an early manager of the Volcano House and a sheriff in Hilo.

Grandma went to the Normal School in Honolulu and after that, took a steamer trip to California and went across country to Kittery, Maine to get her teaching credentials. She stayed with the Maby family in Maine, and then retraced her trip back to Honolulu, where she married Antonio Q. Marcallino.

Great-Grandma Emma Kekaulike Maby

Grandpa Tony had been raised in Honolulu. His parents were from the Azores Islands, in the Atlantic, and were associated with the Portuguese consulate in Honolulu. At one point, Grandpa and his brother Valentine were assigned to take the females of various dignitaries around Honolulu, because it was said that they were "very polite" and "such gentlemen."

Oh, the stories Grandma told. Great-Grandma Pualinui had been a lady-in-waiting to Queen Emma. The queen named my grandmother's baby sister, Laura Kekaulike, a family name. Grandma talked of her brothers, who were assigned stations at the bier when the king died, her siblings and cousins having

Great-Grandpa John Henry Maby

sleepovers in the Palace, and during summer quarters, of picnics at the Royal Court. She told stories of Pualinui's sister, Lahilahi, and all the children she'd had. I later learned that all those children had been adopted.

My sister and I found some of those stories fun, and since I was always interested in food, I'd ask questions:

"What did you eat?"

Grandma would reply, "Sliced tongue."

We'd say, "Ooh, yuck!" I would run to Grandpa, who'd tell me that he was fixing a roast beef for dinner. I was always so relieved it wasn't tongue.

Grandma would have pitchers of lilikoi juice, highly sweetened because it was so tart. We would have guava juice and papaya nectar, and plentiful avocados from the trees on the property. There would be fresh lilikoi chiffon pies from Mike's Café. We'd enjoy eating Chinese food from the Green Garden in Hanapepe. We'd go out for saimin[1] and teriyaki beef sticks. They were a staple in many of the small restaurants, and sometimes we would get plate lunches with potato salad, Spam and rice. Sometimes they'd add a hard-boiled egg. Today it sounds ghastly to me, but back then it was *ono* (yummy).

Great-Grandma Emma with baby Mina

---

[1] A Hawaiian noodle dish similar to ramen.

Summers on Kauai were fun for us. My parents would stick us on a flight to Kauai from Honolulu in June after school was out, and my grandparents would stick us on a flight back to Honolulu when it was time for school to start again. Sometimes my sister Maile and I were permitted to bring a friend, so we brought our neighbor, Linda.

Grandpa would take us around to his Civil Air Patrol meetings and to his Lion's Club meetings at the Kauai Inn in Lihue. He would have lunch with some of his cronies, and we'd have Shirley Temples with little umbrellas at our own table while the grownups gathered at theirs. Sometimes he'd take us up the Wailua River to the Fern Grotto, and back to the Coco Palms for lunch. We went on picnics and spent a lot of time swimming at the Salt Pond. We went to movies in Hanapepe, sitting as far from Grandma as she'd let us. Whenever there was a love scene, we were embarrassed when Grandma would announce, "Oh, they are chewing on each other!"

Caged in the lush back yard of my parents' house in Koloa, Kauai

Almost everywhere we went, we would interact with my grandparents' friends. There were always stories about Grandma being such a strict disciplinarian when she'd been a schoolteacher and principal. People would come up and mention being rapped on their knuckles for misbehavior while their brother or sister might have gotten away with murder. Others would talk about getting the special help they needed when Grandma tutored them. We heard lots of stories about my father, Conway (Muzzy), how he loved to hunt, and the trouble he had gotten into with his cousins at school and having been kicked out several times for pulling pranks.

Always there was the music. Grandma had two or three old-fashioned radios with the huge cabinets and all those tubes. We listened to Hawaiian music and sometimes played music on our ukuleles. We thought nothing of inviting other kids and friends to play with us. Dad had taught us at an early age to play music, and Grandma seemed to enjoy our efforts. Once in a while, if they announced one of the Beamers or another Hawaiian singer, Grandma would say "that's a cousin." We had so many cousins we couldn't keep track of them.

During these summers, Grandma taught me how to sew on her old treadle Singer. I remember tangled threads and feet that didn't catch up with what I was trying to do, but I was happy to be spending time with my grandmother. We had great fun going up to the local grocery store and five-and-dime in the shopping center on the corner—it had everything—we'd buy a few yards of fabric and patterns, and I'd always go back to school with new skirts and dresses. I detested making buttonholes, so Grandma did them for me—then I'd know for sure the buttons would line up correctly. But when I was sewing on my own, I used a lot more hooks and eyes. It seemed natural for me to learn to make my school clothes and muumuus. Once I had a summer job, I spent every paycheck on fabric, zippers, and patterns. We were fortunate to have sewing lessons as part of our home economics classes, which taught me even more as I grew older.

Then there was the cooking. Grandpa Tony was Portuguese, and he fixed beef and pork with vinegar, soy sauce and flaked chili peppers. Sometimes he'd marinate some pork or beef in Worcestershire sauce and garlic. The meats would come out surprisingly tender and flavorful. To this day, I marinate thin pork chops in Worcestershire sauce with garlic, dredge them in flour and fry in butter until brown and done. If the chops are thin, they'll cook very quickly.

Most of our dinners featured rice; rice was almost always served with roasts, chops, barbecued meats, and fish. We had vegetables, too, and I remember bok choy and other oriental veggies on our table. My mother loved artichokes, and they'd have to come from the mainland. And we did have fresh vegetables from our garden and those luscious tomatoes.

Chapter 3

I have more beautiful summer memories. Kauai is known for its lush green foliage, fragrant flowers, and amazingly varied scenes, from the dry leeward side with views of Ni'ihau, to the Waimea Canyon and around the island to the North Shore. The road goes around about two thirds of the island to the cliffs of Napali.

On the southwest side, the road starts at Barking Sands and curves around south, following the coastline to Waimea town, with a road up to Waimea Canyon lookouts and other small towns. My grandparents lived in Eleele, at Port Allen. Further east were Koloa, the Spouting Horn, and homes along the shore at Poipu. There weren't too many touristy things on Kauai back then, but Grandpa knew parks where we could have our picnic

Kauai's North Shore and the Kilauea Lighthouse

lunches. Sometimes he'd hop over a stone wall and come back with a fresh pineapple to cut up for dessert.

Further north along the eastern coastline is the capital of Kauai, Lihue, where the airport is and where the ships brought in goods and people to Nawiliwili Harbor. Following the road and then turning west onto the North Shore brought us to waterfalls, the Wailua River, Hanalei Bay, Lumahai Beach, the Kilauea Lighthouse with its gooney birds,[2] and on to the end of the road to Haena. Just before reaching the road to the lighthouse, there was a lovely, tiny stone church. We always begged Grandpa to stop so that we could visit the little church.

The highway ends at Haena, the beginning of the Napali Coast with its tall cliffs, jungle growth and Kauai red dirt. To access Napali and to go into the valleys, there is a twenty-one-mile trail which is still used today by intrepid hikers who don't

Kalalau Valley

---

[2] The Laysan albatross.

mind some of the sheer drops along the way. The end of the trail will find you in Kalalau Valley, where my family used to hunt. During certain seasons, they could access the valley via boat ride. Over the years, Dad and Grandpa found many artifacts from the Hawaiians who had once lived in the valley. These were donated to the Kauai and Bishop Museums.

Mount Waialeale is at the center of the island and is often called one of the wettest places on earth. It's really a bog of sorts, and the source of many of the falls along the North Shore, as well as the Waimea River which carved out the Waimea Canyon, sometimes called the Grand Canyon of the Pacific. Up past the Waimea Canyon Lookout are the Kalalau Lookout and

Family Cabin, Koke'e. Credit Bob Taylor

some trails. We'd sometimes take picnic lunches up to the picnic tables where we could look over the Kalalau Valley. It's one of the most impressive views on Kauai.

My grandfather had built a hunting cabin up at Koke'e, and it was maintained for a number of years by the family. It was very rudimentary, basically one room and very rustic. After Dad was gone, Maile and her husband put in a few improvements—an outside shower, among them. While we were up there, we'd visit the Waimea Canyon Lookout, have a picnic lunch, go up to the Kalalau Lookout, and enjoy the coolness and the beautiful views. When the state took over the land management, Maile gave up

Waimea Canyon. Credit Bob Taylor

the property. The state wanted a lot of money just to use the cabin a few weeks a year.

An odd thing that tourists don't expect to see are the colorful roosters and the hens alongside the roads up to the lookouts and around the Museum. Today, this feral, interbred chicken variety has become pervasive due to hurricanes in the late twentieth century and to lack of natural enemies. They are loud and sometimes considered a menace, but they are certainly beautiful.

There were a few fields of carnations up alongside the road to the lookouts and the stream that seemed to run uphill. If one was paying attention, one might spot a *pueo*, a Hawaiian owl. There were always wild goats and many times we saw them on impossible pinnacles of rock, looking like statues. There were also axis deer, sheep and boars. Dad and Grandpa had hunted all these animals over the years, and they ate everything they killed.

Sometimes Dad would take a group of kids into the valley to teach them how to live off the land. They'd kill their own meat and learn how to camp, hunt and take care of themselves. In later years, hippies and people who wanted to live off the grid moved into the valley and tried to stake their claims to a part of it. To this day, the state is trying to get some of these people out of the valley. When they leave, they leave behind their trash and quite a few of their belongings. It's a long hike or boat ride back to civilization for doctors and groceries. There are a lot of places to hide from the authorities.

As children, we didn't have to think about hippies or what might happen in the future. We were happy to be with Grandpa and Grandma on our trips up to the canyon. Sometimes we would stop in the town of Waimea and pick up some box lunches; sometimes we'd get fried chicken or bottles of Coke. We loved our picnics.

We spent most of our swimming time at the Salt Pond in Hanapepe. There was a picnic pavilion with adjacent bath and shower rooms. There was a good-sized swimming area with the salt flats off to the side, and a bunch of rocks and boulders delineating the swimming area.

Grandma had a lady friend who was a widow, and sometimes she'd invite Mrs. Pugh to come to our picnics. Mrs. Pugh loved sauerkraut and would usually bring a sauerkraut and hot dog casserole, and we kids didn't care for sauerkraut. But we did like where she lived. Her home was right beside the Hanapepe River where it opened into the bay. The bay water was warm, and the river water was cooler. We often played in the brackish water, liking the contrasts in temperatures. Over the years, some of Mrs.

Hanapepe River

Pugh's yard washed away; I've often wondered how the property looks now, and whether the house is still there.

Upon going home decades later, Maile and I were sorry to see that Mike's Café and the Green Garden restaurants were no longer in business. My grandparents' house, as well as the others in their camp, had been razed, and while we were there, there was only empty acreage. A block from where their house used to be, where we used to climb down the cliffs and swim in the Hanapepe Bay, they had put in a marina. It seemed very strange to be there, and I was glad my sister had accompanied me, because I don't believe I'd ever missed my grandparents and dad more.

To get a taste of home, I started experimenting with different foods and ingredients and found a way to make Chinese pot roast pork or chicken in the slow cooker; I use hoisin sauce, garlic, ginger, and a little brown sugar, with a little gravy flour to thicken the juices. Topping a bowl of rice with the meat and adding some stir-fried pineapple, onion chunks and bell pepper chunks is a delicious meal in a bowl.

Noh, a Hawaiian company, sells packets of Chinese roast pork (charsiu) mix, and even a half-world away, I can find it and order it by the boxful on Amazon. It's a good start to making a marinade for pork and chicken, but I've always added garlic, ginger and brown sugar to the mix for marinating meats. It is worth the extra effort to get that extra taste. Star anise could be another addition to the pot.

Chapter 4

Because of Phylis and her cooking lessons, I grew up with an appreciation of good food. She was a patient woman who took her time talking about and showing me how to cook some of her favorite dishes. She shared recipes, tips and her cookbooks with me. She gave me a sense of achievement and praised me every time the icing for a cake came out smoothly or the barbecue sauce was of the right consistency. Looking back, I probably had as many failures as successes, but she was always encouraging. It wasn't too long before my mother

Barbara Littleton Marcallino— Mom

allowed me to do some of the cooking for our family, and by the time we moved to Kaneohe when I was twelve, I was doing most of the cooking.

Mom had some favorite recipes she'd learned from her mother in California, but really took to Hawaiian and Asian foods, too. The old house in Honolulu had huge rooms, high ceilings and pocket doors. There was a walk-through pantry which was bigger than my kitchen is today. In that pantry were upper and lower cabinets, lots of shelf space and room for an extra refrigerator. How I wish I could have that pantry today, now that I enjoy throwing parties for friends and our big family.

Grandma Mina, pre-marriage

I remember bowls of poi, covered with a little water and kitchen towels draped over the tops to keep out the bugs. There was always a fifty-pound burlap bag of rice on one of the closet shelves, and one or two gallon glass jars of *opihis* (limpets), native to Hawaiian waters. Opihis are a plentiful small shellfish—very salty, but good with rice or poi. Mom used to eat those like candy. We had big canisters for flour, white sugar, and natural brown sugar, from which the molasses had not been removed.

One of my earlier memories was of Mom and Aunt Jeanie mixing some yellow coloring from packets into a big bowl of ghastly white margarine. Butter was hard to come by and expensive, so they went the oleo route. We had a milkman who delivered dairy products a couple of times a week. We never bought too much butter because of the expense (unless I was trying some new recipe that called for it), but we'd always have milk. The milk bottles were layered: liquid on the bottom, cream on the top. We'd have to shake up our milk before pouring it.

When we were on Kauai, Grandma once showed me how to turn our milk into butter in an old jar, by shaking it like crazy. She explained that lots of butter was salted at the dairy and the liquids could be used in place of milk in various recipes. It seemed much easier to go to the dairy case and buy a pound of butter.

I'd find a recipe, and Grandma would help me make it. Sometimes she'd sit at her easel, sketching and gabbing with me while I tried to roll out dough evenly. She and Grandpa always seemed to enjoy my efforts, though some of them left much to be desired. In those early days, maybe a third of my efforts were worth eating. Nowadays I know a lot of ways to make a flop edible, but back then it was hit or miss.

I had my minor disasters, too. I was about nine when I was carrying a pot of barbecue sauce from the stove to the countertop, slipped and flung that whole pot of sauce in an arc around the kitchen. It hit the walls, the worktables, the stove, the sink and the floor! My mom shook her head and said, "Meleana, you have barbecue sauce from hell to breakfast!" (She did help me clean up that mess.) She wasn't so happy that when I made pancakes, I'd always leave one behind the stove for a little field mouse that had made its way inside. I just couldn't help feeding cute little animals even back then.

Poi was a Hawaiian staple and the main starch with every meal. Poi is made from the taro root, which is cooked and then ground down to various consistencies, with water added. It was traditionally eaten with the fingers: Very thick poi was considered "one-finger poi." There was a runnier poi, "two-finger poi" and the runniest, "three-finger poi." Poi is bland and a complement to the saltier fish and pork the Hawaiians ate.

My sister and I liked to play with it, and we'd laugh when newcomers teased us that we were eating library paste. My parents gave us cereal from the mainland sometimes, but much of the time we ate poi for breakfast. Mom made us use a spoon (because we weren't supposed to be *heathens*, for heaven's sake). Our breakfasts consisted of the poi with sugar and milk, maybe a banana or papaya, and every morning, a tablespoon of cod liver oil so we'd be healthy. The oil was almost enough to make us gag.

Once in a blue moon, my mother would get strawberries. My uncle worked for Pan American Airlines and I suspect someone flew them in. Then we'd have a treat for breakfast: Rice Krispies with cream, sugar, and strawberries.

Quite a few of my culinary booboos occurred on Kauai at my grandparents' house. I once put too much milk in a cake recipe. Nowadays you'd call the results a pudding cake or lava cake because the inside was creamy and only just set. It helped that at least it had a firm base and top. Grandma told me not to try to frost it, because it would be gone before the frosting was made. Grandpa had a sweet tooth and ate almost the whole thing.

Grandma also told us kids that we'd have to go in and brush our teeth after any sweets, or we'd end up with false teeth like Grandpa. Then he'd click his teeth in and out and pretend to chase us, and we'd scream and run away from him.

Down the street from our home on Kinau Street in Honolulu was a little grocery store called Henry's Market. We could get some of our groceries there, and Henry cooked certain Japanese foods in the back and sold them by the quart. Mom and I liked his pork tofu, which was basically a Japanese stir fry over rice. He never gave me his recipe, but Phylis taught me how to make it with firm tofu. Back then they took the blocks of tofu out of a vat, and you took them home wrapped in butcher paper, and cooked it immediately. Nowadays tofu comes in its own plastic containers. Henry's dish was made with fresh watercress. We could always find and buy bunches of watercress for next to nothing. I'm guessing that Henry "knew someone" with a stream and grew his own. His pork tofu had the crispiest, most delicious watercress. Tofu is an acquired taste, and to this day, I'm the only one in my family who enjoys it, but the stir fry can be made without it. Sometimes I throw in some soba noodles and a bit of siracha to replace the rice. When I am unable to find fresh oriental-style vegetables, I use canned chow mein veggies and added slivered green onions to the finished dish. For some reason, the green onions make the whole dish taste "fresh."

Like Kauai, Honolulu had its small saimin, cone sushi and teriyaki meat stick carryouts, as well as Chinese takeout places. Sometimes, when my mother didn't feel like cooking, my dad would take us to the Golden Duck for Chinese food. We'd order a number of entrees, they'd bring chopsticks and big bowls of rice, and we'd all share from the various dishes, family style. It took a lot of getting used to, going to most restaurants on the East Coast and ordering just one dish for dinner. When I'm feeding the family, I cook some dishes and order several more takeout, then serve all of the food buffet style. I might make fried rice (Hawaiian fried rice usually has cooked scrambled eggs and slivered meat, chicken or shrimp). On the table might be some of my Chinese roast pork (*charsiu*), stir-fried shrimp and broccoli, or chicken patties with sweet-and-sour sauce, and then whatever we've ordered from the local takeout. A VERY good thing about Asian food is that it always tastes just as good the second day. These days you can find all kinds of Asian sauces, from the various stir-fry sauces to respectable finishing touches. I've used sweet-and-sour, General Tso's, and orange sauce with some good results.

Preparing the meat properly is key. You can cube your chicken or pork, dredge the cubes in corn starch and fry them in hot oil. Drain on paper towels, and the meat is ready to add the sauce of your choice. Coating shrimp like this works too. Cooking at home and using corn starch eliminates and is better than the thick coating on meats served in Chinese takeout. The meat or chicken should be crisp outside and juicy inside, so don't crowd the skillet or wok with too much at a time, or you'll end up with "stewed" meat.

Credit Bob Taylor

Chapter 5

Living on Oahu during the school year and visiting Kauai in the summers kept us busy. When my grandparents came to town, they stayed at the Alexander Young Hotel in downtown Honolulu on Bishop Street. We kids were sometimes allowed to stay with them overnight, and we thought that was a great treat. We loved our downtown excursions with Grandma. We'd go with her down the block and across the street to the bank. Sometimes we'd go across the street to Long's Drugs, and she'd also take us to the Liberty House as well as to the Kress store. Sometimes we'd walk up to St. Andrew's Cathedral to sit in the garden. My sister and I had been christened there and attended Sunday school there. My aunt and uncle were married in the smaller chapel.

Alexander Young Hotel

We'd have lunch at Woolworth's or sometimes at the Kress lunch counter. Grandma would give us a couple of dollars for crayons and coloring books. Sometimes she'd take us to Waikiki to visit a cousin who lived down by the Ala Wai Canal. Beulah lived in a little cottage there, and she and Grandma would gab for hours. She'd give us cookies, but never a whole meal. After visiting, Grandma would take us back to Woolworth's for hamburgers. Once in a while, she'd buy us saimin. Our favorite meals with my grandparents, however, were at the very fancy restaurant at the Young Hotel. We were to use our best manners and had to keep our elbows off the table, because we were "ladies."

Grandma's dentist had an office in the Young Hotel on one of the upper business floors. Her dentist became our dentist. I cannot remember his name, but I remember him telling me that I should study hard and brush my teeth a lot because he knew I would never want to end up like George Washington with wooden teeth! He would tell me stories about the old days, when anyone could become a dentist. In the old days, if teeth were too close together, instead of braces, these charlatans would file between the teeth.

Alawai Canal

After a few stories like that, we thought it smarter to keep our teeth and mouths clean.

Sometimes we got to walk to the Royal Hawaiian Hotel or to the Moana at Waikiki. Grandma enjoyed looking in the shops, but seldom bought anything for herself. My favorite place to shop was the Liberty House, an upscale department store in Honolulu. Every once in a while, Grandma would buy me a new muumuu, and when we started collecting Nancy Ann Story Book Dolls, she'd buy us a doll. Most of our gifts, however, came at Christmas time.

She and Grandpa usually came to town a few days before Christmas and stayed at the hotel, coming to the house to visit, eat and open gifts. The only Christmas trees we could get back then were Cook or Norfolk pines, and we used a lot of tinsel. My mother insisted that we put individual strands on the tree and afterwards, had to remove each strand and store it carefully for the next year. She had special blown ornaments from Mexico and Germany that her mother had given her, and she stored them meticulously in an old suitcase. My favorites were the glass animals with straw tails. I was curious and every year asked the same question: how did the straw get in the glass? I never got an answer, though today I could probably think of a few.

Grandma could bake, but at Christmas time, she always brought the family treats from the bakery at the Young Hotel. She'd bring two or three boxes of pastries: tarts, cookies, eclairs, napoleons, petit fours. They always looked so delicious that it was hard to decide which to choose. We would have a turkey and fixings and those luscious desserts.

Mom and Grandma put us to work in the kitchen. In those days, instant stuffing mix had yet to be developed (Stovetop Stuffing wouldn't be marketed until the 1970s), and everything was made from scratch. Mom would chop onions and celery, and

Grandma, my sister and I would crumble bread that had been dried especially for the stuffing. Sometimes we were tasked with taking the ends and "strings" off the string beans. Sometimes we would help make succotash. We liked corn but didn't like lima beans. On Christmas, we'd have mashed potatoes—one of the few times a year we didn't have rice. Later in life, I learned to make potato dishes, but always preferred rice with my gravy and meat or poultry.

Mom loved oyster dressing so sometimes she'd make a casserole for herself. I don't remember anyone else eating it. Oysters were plentiful enough that she'd fix them in various ways, and she ate them raw, too. She also loved organ meats, including tongue and liver. I was turned off by those foods then, and decades later, I remain so. But I continue to associate oysters with Christmas and my mom's once-a-year treat.

A family favorite was my mother's fruit salad. She would mix canned and fresh fruit—whatever was available. Sometimes there would be very expensive frozen strawberries to add color to the papayas, mangoes, and bananas, perhaps with canned peaches and apricots. Most of the time, however, our fruit salads were tropical. My grandmother loved the addition of canned fruit cocktail, too, and sometimes she'd add a small bottle of maraschino cherries.

These days I use a combination of fresh, canned and frozen fruits and make my salads by the gallon. We can get fresh peaches, pineapples, mangoes, blueberries and strawberries, and adding a little sugar and lime juice brings out the sweetness and tartness of the fruits. Macerating strawberries in a little sugar adds a depth of sweetness to any fruit salad. If the bananas are green when I'm shopping, I might pick up a bag of frozen berries or melon to replace them. In modern supermarkets, so many fruits are available in some form, ready for use, and local farmers markets provide variety as well. Good mangoes can be found in the markets all summer long, but I've not had much luck finding quality papayas. They are usually tasteless, so I've stopped using them.

From mid to late summer, peaches are plentiful on the East Coast, and I've bought them by the case for years. They go into fruit salads, snacks and lots of baking. I've used them in breads, pies, cakes, peach crunch, and just for a bite of "sweet." My husband has a sweet tooth, and the kids and grandkids enjoy peach desserts. I keep homemade streusel topping in the fridge in gallon Ziploc bags for quick desserts.

Phylis had the patience of a saint, teaching me to make pie crusts. She had a lot of patience that I don't have, and once I discovered frozen pie shells, I began making only cookie crumb and butter pressed crusts from scratch. Now, those cookie crusts are available, too! Many of my fruit pies have streusel topping, which means they don't need an upper crust. The streusel makes them a little different in look, flavor and texture.

I'm not always in a hurry and do make fruit breads, cookies, cakes, brownies and pies from scratch. The internet has a lot of interesting recipes and variations from different cultures, and I enjoy reading and learning how different foods are cooked. Sometimes I'll wake with a recipe in my head and try to duplicate it. Sometimes I wish Phylis was still here to critique my efforts, but my husband has been my grateful guinea pig and taste-tester for many years now. The grandkids call him the "Clean-Up Man," and he finishes everything they don't have room for.

Chapter 6

Hawaii is known for its warm, loving people. People who travel to the islands from the mainland and all over the world are not only impressed by the climate and lovely scenery of the mountains and ocean, but also by the "aloha spirit" and generosity of the Hawaiians they meet. Many *malihinis* (visitors) come back time and again to enjoy the ambiance, friendship and casual lifestyle.

It's something I didn't much think of until I was older, but we grew up with a sense of acceptance and *hanai*, a word which roughly means "adoption." When you loved someone—a neighbor, a single parent, an acquaintance—you automatically accepted them as one of the family. You invited them in to eat with you, gave them a bed or a cot if they needed a place to sleep. We both "adopted" friends and neighbors and were the recipients of hanai when our home burned down when I was sixteen.

After the fire, my friend Pat and her parents took me in, threw me a "clothing shower" and took care of me while I finished out the school year and until I could move back in with my family. I lived with them in Kaneohe and was astounded when I came home from church and half my class was there, throwing me a shower which replenished my wardrobe. All the clothing and footwear I could ever use was presented to me. The mothers had sewn most of my new wardrobe. I had nightwear, blouses, skirts, shirtwaist dresses, muumuus, slips, underwear, flip flops, shoes

and sweaters. Only the sweaters, underwear and footwear were bought. In those days, we made most of our own clothing. Judging from the sheer volume, the women had worked around the clock to pull off my party. They took the time to prepare the foods, desserts and drinks that they served. I'll never forget their kindness, and my friends at school were happy to see me wearing their contributions. When my grandparents came to Honolulu to take us shopping, they bought me a new swimsuit and glasses. That was all I needed.

I was grateful for such kindness and largesse. I don't think it dawned on me that my family was just as generous as those who were so good to me. My parents accepted everyone, and everyone was welcome at our table. Grandma was very Victorian and straitlaced, but her heart was as big as all outdoors. She and Grandpa encouraged us to "bring friends" and were always helping people out. It wasn't something that people did for recognition, but for the joy of helping and making new friends.

Someone would have to be really awful for their calls for help to be ignored; otherwise, people gave according to their strengths. If you had knowledge, you taught or tutored. If you could sew, you made things for someone who couldn't. If you could cook, you'd volunteer to cook for the Chinese widow next door or for PTA meetings and bake sales. In short, willingness to help others while enjoying their company was characteristic of the Hawaiians of my youth. No one was a stranger for long.

Phylis had shown kindness and patience in teaching a hyperactive little girl to cook. Several other neighbors would later encourage me in my baking efforts, and one even ate some cake with blue frosting. Now, when I think of how awful that cake looked, I marvel that Mrs. McCully could stomach it. She lent me cake pans sometimes when I was experimenting, and she kindly let me pass through her property to get to the big fig tree in the next yard down the hill. I could climb that tree with a favorite book and lose myself for a while, and it was nice that she always had books for me to borrow.

Grandma taught me some of life and society's grand essentials; one of those was writing "pleases and thank-yous." One had to be polite! If someone invited you somewhere, it was polite to write a thank-you note for the outing. If someone passed away, it was polite to write a letter of condolence to their relatives. If you received a gift at a party or in the mail, a thank-you letter was required. Grandma liked receiving letters and hearing from her friends, and she taught me to love letter-writing, too. She'd earlier taught me to read, a job in itself since I was dyslexic. She encouraged me to find pen pals, and before I knew it, I was writing to pen pals in the north of England and in France. I still enjoy writing letters, but most of them are on the internet nowadays, although there is a stationery box in my desk for those letters which must be personal and hand-written.

There were so many ethnicity and race combinations all living on the islands. Perhaps there was discrimination among the races, but we kids didn't notice much of it. Being *hapa* (mixed) ourselves, we accepted everyone who accepted us. Grandma complained about the newcomers who were taking over the islands, but she had friends of all races and nationalities, as did Grandpa. On a trip home after their deaths, I was pleasantly surprised by the mix of people who came to talk to us about them and their impacts on their lives.

We were raised to be kind and to consider other people's feelings. I remember being angry at a boy who sat in front of me at school. He'd done something I didn't like, and Grandma told me that maybe he'd had a bad day, so try to be nice to him. Kindness begets kindness.

As an adult, too, I never had problems making friends, and could talk to just about anyone, much to my loved ones' surprise.

As strange as it seems, people come up and talk to me in all sorts of venues. I can be at a fruit stand or in line at the bookstore. My family and I have eaten dinner in a restaurant and had a complete stranger come up, put her arm around me and talk to me. (My husband told my daughter that "that always happens with your mother!") My attitude towards people today is a result of my Hawaiian upbringing: if one is pleasant and welcoming, half the battle is won. Doing my charity work, baking for fundraisers, sewing quilts for new babies, is just something I do. It's sometimes surprising to get thanks for something that is so much fun.

Grandpa Tony with the Territorial Legislature

I've taught several people to speak English and helped them pass tests for employment. That was fun, too. I can't say that I learned much Portuguese or Urdu in the process, but I made some friends for life. I have no idea how I did it. Hanai works its magic. While taking on their communication needs, I have gained a best friend, a new brother, and an Afghani son who's gifted me with joy via two more grandchildren to spoil. Life is very strange, and it's easy to wonder what my parents and grandparents would think of how we turned out and how their teaching had influenced us.

Grandma would be pleased that I'm still writing letters and remembering my pleases and thank-yous. Grandpa would be tickled that I love politics. He was the representative to the Territorial Legislature from Kauai for a few years. I think they'd both be happy that their three grandchildren made happy lives with lots of friends, partly because of their love and guidance.

Chapter 7

The Hawaiians of old were spiritual. Most people believed in the Missionary God as well as the "gods of nature." Grandma was of two minds. She'd speak of God sometimes, and of "being good," and when she talked about the old gods, she showed us that she was also superstitious. She always told me too, that she "knew things." That was before *The Twilight Zone*, but I knew she believed it, and in time, I believed it, too. There were stories we all learned in Sunday school: *Daniel in the Lion's Den*, *Noah and the Ark*, and *Jonah and the Whale*. She'd sing us songs like "Jesus Loves the Little Children." Then at home there would be stories about Madame Pele, Goddess of the Volcano, the *Menehune* (Little People), and the legends of Maui.

Grandma sometimes took us to church during our summer visits. She attended a little Congregational church in Hanapepe. I don't remember much about the services, but I do remember the singing. The hymns were a mix of contemporary and old, sometimes in Hawaiian and sometimes in English. After church, we'd usually go to the Green Garden or Mike's Cafe for lunch.

Hanapepe was a small town with a couple of churches, shops and the movie theater, and we'd run into our grandparents' and Dad's friends everywhere. People would get together and "talk story." Some of these stories were a mix of true and fabricated local gossip, and there were exaggerations, too. The tales would be about how many fish Kimo caught spearfishing or how many boyfriends Leimomi kept on the string. Nothing was particularly mean-spirited, but if the stories were racy and kids were around, there might be more suggestive gestures and fewer words. Many of these stories were in pidgin English, and a few had references to the gods.

Grandpa loved to tell us stories of the Menehune who had settled Kauai before the Hawaiians came and had built the fishpond in Lihue. The Menehune were men of small stature who could accomplish fantastic feats overnight, building their structures and walls out of lava rock. The fishpond was built over a thousand years ago, to raise fish to feed the *ali'i*, or chiefs.

When Grandma Mina talked about growing up on the Big Island, she'd describe Puna, her grandmother's birthplace, and Hilo. She'd talk about the volcano and Volcano House where her dad was manager, and she'd talk about Pele, the goddess of the volcano. Grandma had at least two pictures of Halemaumau Crater. One was a particularly striking illustration with the queen giving food and liquor sacrifices to Madame Pele in the volcano. It wasn't unusual for Pele to meet travelers along the road and hitch a ride up the mountain. Sometimes she'd appear as an old woman, and other times as a beautiful young

Conway "Muzzy" Marcallino—Dad 1970s

girl. She was said to entice lovers, and heaven help those who spurned her. Earthquakes and eruptions would follow if she was displeased.

Dad was the consummate storyteller. He had a radio show in Honolulu which was on in the mornings. He usually gave it in pidgin English, taking Anglo children's stories and telling them Hawaiian style. He also wrote stories about some of the Hawaiians of legend and our love for the land. We loved his stories as they were full of spoonerisms as well as variations—the big bad wolf became the big wild *puaa* (boar), for example—and it was just fun to listen. I think Dad loved his pidgin as much as Grandma liked being the perfect lady who spoke very perfect English.

Dad related to us the legend of the *aweoweo*, a red fish. Legend was that they came close to shore to take the ali'i's spirit back to Tahiti after death. He also spoke about the Night Marchers, warrior spirits who marched at night to pay homage to the gods. One must not look at them and must prostrate until they passed. Ti plants were supposed to be planted around a home to protect it from these spirits. People who happened to look upon them would only be spared if they had a relative among the marchers. Dad also talked of a "whistling wind" which presaged the death of an ali'i. He told us stories about Mano the shark and Maui, the god, or demi-god in some Polynesian cultures. He talked of shooting stars appearing when the ali'i died and the legend of Kauai's Koolau the Leper.

When I was older, Grandma started telling me about the women in her family. Descending from old royalty, she cautioned that one had to be proper and not discuss family history with strangers.

Perhaps the call for secrecy was driven by a sense of intrigue. Children were not encouraged to ask questions, and Grandma had always regretted not finding out more about her lineage. She told me many stories about her grandparents, her mother Emma, and the palace. Sometimes I thought that for someone who wasn't supposed to talk about royalty, she sure did it a lot. Later in life, she was able to verify oral family history through the Bishop Museum and genealogy experts, as well as extended family. I found her stories were intriguing because of the bits of superstition thrown in here and there. Her beliefs were evident in her anecdotes and were just a part of who she was. She'd tell me stories about her sisters and cousins at Kamehameha School and going to the palace for sleepovers. She'd talk of some of the women in the lineage who were prescient and knew when certain events would occur, sometimes as much as a year ahead of time. For her part, Grandma herself

Muzzy and Mina Marcallino—Dad and Grandma, 1960s

would dream of events or of friends going through deaths in the family on another island, and would later describe it as if she'd been there.

When my infant son died a crib death and we returned to Hawaii to bury him, my dad told me that Grandma had known that something was wrong (all she'd had was a picture I'd sent her) and was waiting for the call. After she died, I found the picture with these words she'd written on the back: "This baby doesn't look like he's long for this world."'

Strange things happen in life. Perhaps some are coincidences and perhaps not. When Grandma died and Dad was closing her house, a Hawaiian came to the back door and told him that "the aweoweo were running." Dad walked the short walk to the bay and the water was red with the little fish. It was comforting to hear that Grandma had gone home. When Dad died, shooting stars were seen by his grandsons at the moment he passed. Strange as it seems, back here on the East Coast, a daughter and I, unbeknownst to each other months before, had told others close to us that we knew Dad (her grandfather) would die on Thanksgiving. He did. I'd been expecting the call and was not surprised when it happened. Grandma called this sense "the knowing," or in her case, simply "dreams." I cannot explain our awareness, but I can tell you that they have occurred in our family in more than one generation of women.

Chapter 8

It was Saturday morning and time to go to choir practice. The church's window shutters were lifted and opened, and there were a few bugs on the screens. The church interior gratefully received the trade winds—no air conditioner was needed in this little white church in Hawaii. Listening to the harmonies coming from the choir brought us joyful uplift, and singing with our friends offered even more. We enjoyed our singing and our friends and also enjoyed the gold pews, the dozens of poinsettias at Christmas time, all arranged around the altar. During the rest of the year, the floral arrangements were gorgeous and plentiful. Growing up, I enjoyed going to church, mainly for the music, but I also loved the ambiance and the Bible stories.

One Hawaiian may sing a song. Two or more Hawaiians sing in harmony, and put a bunch of them together, and you have a choir *and* a party. The sounds at St. Andrews Cathedral were richer and louder and more contained than in our usual little church, with microphones helping to amplify the sounds within its stone walls. Dad and Grandma sang the hymns along with us kids, and we went home for lunch quite happy. My favorite song was "Onward, Christian Soldiers," but I also loved the hymns sung in Hawaiian.

Both Dad and Grandma encouraged us to sing, and they sang with us. When we were about eight or nine, Dad started teaching us to play the ukulele. We'd play simple songs, and he'd sing with us. When we became more proficient, he'd switch to harmony, and we'd go through various songs, from simple, silly kid songs to "Hawaiian Wedding Song." When friends were over, Dad taught them how to play, too. He had a tenor guitar which

King Kamehameha statue

he named Venus because of her shape![3] He told me that Grandma also had played the guitar, but I don't remember seeing her with one, except in an old picture. I was absolutely thrilled when he gave me Venus.

    Dad loved the land and the Hawaiian people and wrote poetry and prose about both. In college, he'd started putting some of his poetry to music. He loved to play with his friends, and sometimes he performed impromptu at the hotel bars with his friends and entertainers. Some Sundays, he took us with him

---

[3] A tenor guitar is slightly smaller than a six-string guitar and is tuned and played like a ukele. –Ed.

to the Moana Hotel and the Banyan Court, and he'd play music for the mainland audience on "Hawaii Calls." Dad knew Webley Edwards, the producer, and taught the performers some of his original music. He also enjoyed teaching us a drinking song or two that he'd written in college. My favorite is about Lehua "who looks mo' bettah when she hulas in her sweatah." I've been known to sing it to my grandchildren after a piña colada or two.

Dad seemed to know everyone. He loved to attend parties with my mother, and sometimes they'd take us kids along with

Visitors from the mainland! This photograph was taken after Uncle Phil and Auntie Jeanie's wedding (left). Mom and Dad in the center, Maile front center, Grandma Bessie, me, and Grandpa Steve. This was at the house on Kinau Street.

them. We kids would find other kids, enjoy ourselves and make our own mischief. I can remember various friends, various houses, (the ones with the swimming pools or the beach outside were great!), various foods. While the parents were playing music and drinking Primo Beer, we could be found swimming, playing games, or outside up the hill, making a fort out of banana leaves. A favorite pastime was hunting for centipedes. We'd get jars and go hunting under rocks and steppingstones. Mom would make us set them free, far from the house, and then she'd tell us it was time to go to bed. So someone would find us a bed, and we'd go to sleep until our parents were ready to take us home.

Usually several hours later, Dad would come in and say, "Come on kids. It's time to go home. It's getting dark!" Well, it could be 10:00 pm or 4:00 am or the sun could be rising, and it was always the same. All it meant was that it was late and time to go home. To this day, when it's time to *pau hana* (quit work), or stop what we're doing, I use Dad's phrase, "It's getting dark!"

Dad liked to take us around with him out on jobs or crabbing, and he liked to take our friends, too. We'd all sit in the back of the car and play our ukuleles and sing our hearts out. Dad would be in the front seat harmonizing with us or teaching us new words. Some of his drinking songs were risqué, some were traditional, some were Hawaiian. My friends still remind me of the fun we had back then, with our ukes and our music and Dad.

In Kaneohe, one of my parent's favorite hangouts was Honey's Cafe. It was a small eatery and bar on the main highway, and not too far from our house. This establishment was owned by Sunny and Honey Ho, the parents of entertainer Don Ho. My parents would take my baby brother with them to the bar, and he grew up learning to talk with a pet myna bird. We'd also met other singers and celebrities over the years, and at the time thought nothing of it.

Years later, when Dad was sick, I went home to visit him for a month. I took along Wanda, my sister-in-law. Since it was her first trip to Hawaii, we took a number of tours and short trips to the outer islands so that she could see as much as possible. Her main wish was to see Don Ho's floor show. As usual, it was a colorful production, full of song, harmonizing and hula, and afterwards, it was my pleasure to introduce her to him. His words to me were "you look like a local girl." I said I was Muzzy's daughter "grown up," and that he'd met me years ago in his parents' bar. We went on from there. Wanda told me later that having her picture taken with Don Ho was the highlight of her trip. What I enjoyed most were the familiar music, singing along, and the feeling of finally being home. The fact that I remembered the hula motions was amusing, too. Today, while my mind is

Halona Blowhole, a popular tourist destination on Oaho

young and I can still sing (kinda), my body no longer cooperates, and I'd be hard pressed to dance the simplest hula.

We had a variety of foods at my parents' friends' parties. There would be traditional American party foods, or *luau* foods such as kalua pig, poi, *laulaus*, lomi salmon and *haupia*, a coconut pudding dessert. We might have grilled fish (usually swordfish or mahimahi) and other seafood, or teriyaki chicken or steak.

Sometimes my mother made cioppino, a seafood stew, which she loved although it was a production to prepare. We kids would eat anything, and we loved hamburgers and hot dogs. There would be macaroni salad and fruit salads or trays. Appetizers might be shrimp, a vegetable tempura with dipping sauce, or a platter of *charsiu* (Chinese roast pork-thinly sliced and served cold with scallions). Other platters might contain *sashimi*, (sliced raw ahi tuna or other fish), *opihi* (limpets), and various kinds of sushi rolls made with pickled rice, seaweed, veggies and eel or

Credit Fithree Hadiwiyono

fish. The raw fish was always served with dips, one of them hot oriental mustard.

Cioppino is basically an Italian seafood stew, consisting of crab, shrimp, firm fish, scallops, mussels, clams, and lobster, all cooked in a tomato base, to which wine is added. This stew was messy to eat, and if you got it at Fisherman's Wharf, it was served with a bib. At home, Mom didn't make it often, but if she did, she intended to eat it, and I don't remember much sharing. The stew was served with fresh sour dough bread for dipping and sopping up the juices. She had a friend who made huge pots of cioppino for parties sometimes; I remember her face and her house, but not her name. We loved those parties up on Tantalus Drive on the side of the mountain, because while the adults were eating, drinking and playing music, we kids would be outside on the mountain exploring, building forts and playing "king on the hill."

Many of the parties were potluck, which was more affordable for young families. Veggie and fruit trays were always popular. Mom's contribution to the veggie tray was always celery, with the strings removed, filled with a mixture of cream cheese and mayo, and sprinkled with paprika. She'd also add black and green olives. The fruit trays consisted of various fruits, maybe served with a sweet, creamy dip. The dip ingredients were cream cheese, cream, sugar and mayo, sometimes with orange or lemon juice and zest added to give it some zing. It was good enough that we kids would want to eat it with a spoon. On those trays, the staples were bananas, mangoes and fresh pineapple, and everything extra was a treat. We were happy now and then to find grapes, strawberries and sometimes melon. Over the holidays, the grocery stores always had small mandarin oranges by the case, so we'd be sure to look on the table for a bowl of those with a discard bowl for the rinds right next to it.

Chapter 9

Fun. Happiness. Joy of living. Sometimes sadness and grief. Everyone experiences these feelings during their childhood. Sometimes kids worry about grades, or their parents and siblings. There are divorces and deaths in the family as well as celebrations of life, births, and holidays. With these milestone highs and lows that anchor our individual timelines, there are the common, mundane occasions that fill up the spaces in between: work and church, both fulfilling and deficient family and friend connections, and for kids, schoolwork and chores.

Honolulu Museum of Art

Dad helped to make our childhood fun, and I find that the fun times come to mind more frequently than the sad times. In a lot of ways, Dad was like a big kid. He could be serious, but he did love his music and taking us along with him to work, parties and to some of his weekend music gigs. Before teaching us to play the ukulele and guitar, he'd take us with him to the hotels and bars where he would meet his friends, have a few Primos and play his music. While he was "busy," we'd make our own fun. After he'd taught us to play music, he STILL took us with him. We met all sorts of local celebrities and thought nothing of it. We played our ukes in the car and always enjoyed the trip as much as the destination.

If Dad and friends were playing music at the bar besides the pool at a hotel down at Waikiki, we kids would be learning to swim. When I was five or six, he threw me in the pool, telling me that if I wanted to go surfing with him, I'd have to learn how to swim first! Consequently, I learned quickly. We were water rats, and we always managed to end up in the water, wherever we went.

Queen's Surf was one of Spencecliff's restaurants down at the end of Waikiki. The restaurant had a beautiful building with an extensive Japanese garden and a koi pond. You could cross cement steppingstone pillars to a small island with all sorts of miniature trees and a stiff oriental grass. There were little stone statues and lit lanterns and the "moat" was full of colorful koi. Around the perimeter of the garden were lit tiki torches. The outside dining area looked out on the ocean and the garden. Dad and Mom would be occupied with their friends, and sometimes with the entertainment, while we kids played in the garden.

If there was a body of water, I'd invariably fall into it. I can remember falling in the moat, wiggly koi around my legs, and then drying off, wearing the head chef's T-shirt, sitting on a stool in the kitchen, chomping on a prime rib bone. That was great fun!

Mom would scold me for getting wet and say "Marian, Marian, quite the contrarian!" and I would think I was someone special. (And I loved prime rib bones.)

The Honolulu Academy of Arts[4] was a block away from our house, and across the street from that was Thomas Square Park, which took up the whole block. In that beautiful park were paths, many banyan trees, and in the center, a huge round pool with a fountain. We'd dip our feet in the pool and try to play house in the many roots of the banyan trees. The little "rooms" made wonderful forts and houses.

When Dad bought us our first bicycles, he took us to Thomas Square to teach us to ride. He thought it would be safer than teaching us on the sidewalks in front of the house, alongside our busy street. I loved my bike, and Dad didn't curse very often, but he did curse the day I thought it would be fun to ride on the stone lip of the Thomas Square fountain, and fell in with my brand new bike, head over teacup.

Across the street from Thomas Square, we attended Lincoln Elementary School, also known as Linekona School. One of the features was a big tubular slide on the side of the main building, which was the school's fire escape. The slide extended from the ground up to the second floor. Sometimes we'd go climb up that tube so we could slide down. We were not supposed to be there!

We had a lot of fun at the house, too. Dad loved to hunt, and this is how we happened to have a pet baby goat. Dad had gone to Kauai for his usual hunting trip and killed a nanny goat up on a ridge. When he climbed there to retrieve his kill, he found her kid cowering in the brush. He put that kid into his jacket and took care of her, and when it was time to come home, he brought the baby back with him on the mail plane.

---

[4] Now the Honolulu Museum of Art.

He and Mom named our goat "Sweet Pea," and she was a joy to play with. She was energetic, loved to hop and climb and was very friendly. She loved everyone, and she was house trained. We had Sweet Pea while Dad had his morning radio show. A local celebrity, J. Akuhead Pupule, (Hal Lewis) had his own program, and he and Dad were friends. *Aku* is a fish, and *pupule* is "crazy" in Hawaiian, so basically J. Akuhead Pupule means "J. Crazy Fish-head." J Aku was noted for his antics and sense of humor. He loved being the center of attention and planning publicity stunts to promote his program.

When I was four or five, he was visiting and had some fun with Sweet Pea, holding me on his knee while he teased both me

Thomas Square Park Fountain, Honolulu

and the goat. In those days at the movie theaters, short feature films preceded the main attraction. J. Aku thought that he, Sweet Pea, and I should be in a short movie, also, to be played at the closest theater. I do not remember who eventually had the honor of filming it, but I do remember the event.

On a bright sunny day, J. Akuhead, Sweet Pea, and I were filmed down at Kapiolani Park by the zoo at the far end of Waikiki. It was very silly, but the premise of the piece was that the goat was attacking me (Sweet Pea was actually eating the hibiscus out of my hair), so J. Aku had to save me. The rest of the movie consisted of J. Aku chasing Sweet Pea around the park with a big net at the end of a long pole. J. Aku was long and skinny and was wearing shorts. He was the caricature of a mad hunter/scientist. Sweet Pea loved to run and jump and be chased, so this was right up her alley.

The whole thing was ridiculous, and my mother told me it was just one of Akuhead's pranks, but the short played at the Palace Theater for a while. Dad took us kids and some friends to see his daughter "da movie star." It was a short-lived career for me, but I remember the events fondly. I loved my new dress and enjoyed being the center of attention for a while until J. Aku began chasing our goat. I remember the children's laughter when Sweet Pea jumped and hopped and looked over her shoulder to see how close J. Aku was. Then he jumped and hopped, too, mimicking her actions.

Sweet Pea eventually died from eating something she shouldn't have, and we were sad to lose her. We did have the other pets: Bolo the boxer, Michael the terrier, and several cats. At the time, we'd listen to the radio programs, and we'd get *Boston Blackie*, *The Green Hornet*, *The Lone Ranger* and other shows. Our cats were named Boston Blackie, Inspector Faraday, Mary Wesley, Tonto and other radio character names. My mom's favorite cat was called "Man-Cat" because Mom said he was "endowed." We kids didn't know what "endowed" meant. Man-Cat outlived many of our pets and was my mother's companion for a long time. We had chickens and rabbits as well as our pets; Dad would take care of feeding the chickens and rabbits, and we kids put down water and food for the dogs and cats.

Our parents had a wide circle of friends and we had many visitors from the mainland at various times. The circus would come to Honolulu. Dad's good friend was Homer Snow, and he usually worked in the San Diego Zoo. One year, he accompanied the circus for some reason, and he was in charge of the pelicans and seals. When this circus wagon mysteriously showed up in our driveway, before we knew it, there were three large tubs of water in our front yard, with a seal in each tub. On the sides of the tubs were stands, on which stood some pelicans. I remember Homer telling us kids, "A mighty fine bird is a pelican—his beak can hold more than his belly can!" We thought that was funny and never forgot it.

Homer proceeded to put on a show for us, with barking seals and the pelicans catching fish and jumping from tub to tub. Every kid in the neighborhood showed up for the show. Mom brought out sandwiches, and the guys and parents sat around and drank beer. Imagine the excitement of having the circus right in your front yard! Later in the afternoon, before Homer left to join the rest of the circus, he and Dad got a little sloshed. Homer decided he wanted to kiss our maid, Becky. She said no, and of course he went on to chase her, and she took off down the street, Homer in hot pursuit. I don't remember if he ever caught her, but I do remember all of us kids chasing the two of them around the block. Something like that would never happen today.

There were many other parties at the house and at friends' homes. Sometimes Phylis would cook food for our parties, helping Mom out, who was also cooking. The Weavers would bring big boxes of lobster, which we'd cook and serve with drawn butter and Phylis's melt-in-your-mouth dinner rolls. There would be fresh produce and those luscious tomatoes from our garden. Nine times out of ten there was fresh fruit and juice for a sweet treat, but if we were lucky, there was ice cream in the freezer. And there'd be cases of Primo beer.

Grandma had furnished the large rooms of the old-fashioned Victorian with antique, oversized marble-topped pieces, huge bookcases, and hutches with mirrors and lots of carvings. Most of the adults would be out on the big front porch or in the front yard and we kids would play in the house. Hide-and-seek was our typical game. My sister Maile loved to hide in the top of the old upright piano, which no longer played. I liked to hide in the big bookcase or the bottom shelf of the china cabinet. The Weaver kids would hide, too, and Billy would sometimes sneak outside and hide in Michael's doghouse. Other playmates were the Hemmings, and I recall Fred Jr. hiding in Dad's closet where he stored his hunting rifles.

With such fun playmates and lots of play time, we kids always had a ball and ran wild, but we seldom got into real trouble with our parents. We knew our parameters and obeyed our parents' rules. We did our homework and chores. Those were the days of lessons, where most parents took the time to teach their kids table manners and how to treat people, and taught by example. My grandparents were great teachers, too. We kids didn't want to disappoint our elders, so most of the trouble we stumbled into was minor and "kid stuff," and our infractions were dealt with quickly and forgotten.

Phylis sometimes made pies for our family parties, just as she did for Fisherman's Wharf. Apple and blueberry were the most prevalent, due to the long life of both blueberries and apples. I don't recall her making any tropical fruit pies, or chiffon pies as Grandma did. Her sauces were delicious, and we'd be sure to have ice cream on hand if she said she'd be bringing over some homemade caramel or chocolate sauce. My favorite thing was Phylis's homemade cream puffs. She'd serve them with sweetened whipped cream and dust them with powdered sugar. I later found a French cream recipe that I now use in my cream puffs and for cream pie filling. The vanilla cream is easily converted to chocolate, coconut, maple or banana cream for pies. For a piña colada pie, I put a can of pineapple pie filling in the baked crust, and then add the coconut pie filling and whipped topping.

Chapter 10

Kids grow, and we Marcallino kids thrived. When our parents divorced and went on to new lives, we kids were split up. My sister and brother lived in California, and I elected to stay in Hawaii. My teen years were interesting and busy, and I had a great time pursuing my passions.

For a number of years, I took classes at the Art Academy and enjoyed them thoroughly. I loved illustrating, designing clothing, and interior design. I learned to work with color and to appreciate our bright heritage of colors of the islands. My grandmother financed my classes, which I took after school. She encouraged me to apply what I'd learned to everyday living, and it was fun for me to decorate rooms, to choose colors and textures and to make interesting tableaus. I learned to make changes to basic sewing patterns to design different styles of clothing. I found that I could create new combinations of food and make up recipes, and later found that I could market some of my creations so that they would sell. I listened to Grandma when she told me to put "my art" into everything I did.

As a teenager, I started making jewelry, which I sold for pin money. In those days, you could go to Woolworth's and buy all kinds of natural things in their crafts department. I'd buy the hardware and make earrings, necklaces and bracelets out of dyed shells and shark teeth. All I had to do was wear a pair of the earrings to school and someone would want to buy them.

In school, I volunteered to make the signs for our school functions, and I enjoyed doing that. At some of the functions, I would bake cookies or cakes for the refreshment tables and would be responsible for designing the layout, with the moms who were helping. In those days, student functions were handled by the students with parental supervision. It was a responsibility not to be taken lightly.

Summers on Kauai found me painting often with my grandmother. With her encouragement, I found painting with Grandma fun and satisfying enough for me to want to continue from year to year. I tried to do at least one painting each summer.

At one point, Dad had a photography tour business, and he hired Hawaiian models to pose for his mainland tourists at some of the famous tourist spots. These models' pictures ended up in advertisements and calendars, and besides modeling, these ladies had other jobs; they were mothers, secretaries, teachers, and entertainers.

Lani was such a model, a beautiful, graceful woman, who danced with a hula troupe for her main source of income. Dad had tried, without success, to get us to hula. He'd sent us to hula lessons at the YWCA, but Sis and I always had more fun in their big pool swimming, after cutting class. At some point, Lani came along, and she had the patience to teach me to hula. In those days I could bend my knees properly, paying attention to "always raise your elbows" and "don't flap your hands—they are graceful and expressive—use them!" which were words I learned to obey. At one point, I could do a passable hula, enough to dance at parties and with other dancers at shows.

Two boys from high school heard me playing Venus, my guitar, handed down from Dad. They were forming a trio and wanted me to join them to perform folk music. I loved the melodies and harmonies of folk music; I loved playing in the group. After much practice, we were asked to play at the YMCA for the sailors and airmen who were stationed or on leave in Hawaii. We high school kids were just one of the groups entertaining the troops. We also played two or three times at a small coffee house in Honolulu before it went out of business, and I really didn't care at the time, for I'd discovered "BOYS!"

Earning money was essential, and besides a few minor "entertainment" engagements, I earned my money after school and at summer jobs. One summer while staying with my grandparents, I worked at the pineapple cannery on Kauai. Sometimes I babysat for friends of the family. One summer I worked as a babysitter for expecting mothers before their babies were due. I'd watch their kids at home, cook meals and help out before and after the mom and new baby came home from the hospital. Sometimes the moms would want to "keep me" for the summer, and I always turned them down. I had to go to Kauai to see my grandmother while I could. Grandpa Tony died when I was sixteen.

Some of Dad's friends worked for the hotels, and if tourists could afford to bring their families to stay in these fabulous suites, they could afford a seasoned babysitter. I would frequently be called to sit with kids at the hotels, and that earned me a lucrative wage and high tips. Dad would take me to the hotel, make sure everything was on the up-and-up, and pick me up afterwards. I spent a lot of time at the hotels on school-year weekends. I had fun with the kids and ordering room service when they wanted to eat something. Had I been babysitting in someone's home, *I'd* have been the cook and the room service.

I was not driving, myself. My one and only road lesson added to Dad's baldness, or so he said! I had been practicing on my grandmother's old car with a stick shift, and I was forever grinding gears. He came to Kauai on a business trip and decided it was time I learned to drive. I managed to drive from Port Allen at Grandma's to Waimea town and back. Dad asked me to pull into the Green Garden parking lot. Unfortunately, I hit the gas instead of the brake, and managed to run down some hibiscus bushes and a few outside tables and chairs. It was fortunate that no customers were sitting in them! That was it for Dad. "No more!" said Dad, and he meant it. I didn't learn to drive until I was thirty-six and had five children. And no, I didn't try to teach them to drive!

My teen years weren't just school and work. I had cousins to "run with," my best friend Carolyn, and family friends who owned and kept a horse at the stables down by the Honolulu Zoo. Karen loved her horse and sometimes we'd go to the stables and ride Noni, curry her, and practice our bareback riding around Kapiolani Park. I wasn't too tall, so I had to climb on a fence to be able to get on Noni's back. It was a great thrill to ride and canter around the park and to take care of a horse! Afterwards, Karen and I would go across the street to the Natatorium, which was a memorial to soldiers. We'd swim there, daring each other to jump from the various high dives. Sometimes Karen would borrow a friend's horse and we'd gallop around the park together. I never fell off Noni, although I came close a few times. It's amazing how resilient and fearless kids are.

I was still making my own clothing, and horseback riding and swimming are two different sports. I had to be covered for the horseback riding, so I ended up designing and making a shorter muumuu with slits up the side to wear over my swimsuit for riding and for the bus trip to and from the stables. I'd just take it off for the swimming. Many of my outfits growing up were for multiple purposes, namely, swimming and *anything* else. We always had a bathing suit top under our clothes, just in case we found some water that went begging for swimmers. I imagined that I looked like a "Wild Indian" riding Noni, with my bare legs hugging her sides, barefooted and my hair streaming behind me. Perhaps I'd seen too many movies?

Carolyn and I were best pals—we'd met in second grade at the Lincoln Elementary School and worked together in the cafeteria. Back then, the kids all had revolving cafeteria duty.

Some worked in the kitchen, some dished out the lunches, some washed dishes. We all had to take our turns, and the duty was mandatory. Caro was soon spending time at our home, and I at theirs, and we became lifelong friends. When my mom moved with my brother and sister back to the mainland, I spent so much time at Caro's house that I started calling her mom, Mora, "Mom." After my parent's divorce, I lived with them for about six months.

Kapiolani Park, by C. H. Graves, 1902.

Caro's house was also an old Victorian, on the lower slopes of Tantalus. We would go to school and come home together, leaving our homework until later. We'd put on shirts over our swimsuits and take off with our roller skates down the hill and end up at the Punahou School. Their music hall had a lovely cement courtyard, perfect for skating. Sometimes we'd find a store where we'd buy teriyaki meat sticks and cone sushi and have an early dinner. We wouldn't go home until it was almost dark.

Other times, we'd cut through yards and make our way downhill, all the way to the water company fountain at the foot of the mountain. It was much too shallow for swimming, but we HAD to get wet! We'd follow the stream up the mountain, playing in the little pools and climbing, always climbing over the rocks. We loved the cool algae and water. We found an old rock quarry where they processed rocks for driveways, and although it could have been dangerous, we'd climb to the tops of the stacks and slide down, getting little rocks in our swimsuit bottoms. We had "forts" built in various areas where wild fig trees grew. Caro's mom worked outside the home and never knew what we were really doing. As long as we were home by dinnertime and got good grades, she never seemed to worry about us.

    Caro's mom had a friend out in the country, and sometimes on weekends we'd all go to visit. While the elders gabbed and caught up with each other, we kids would walk up the road to the sugar cane field and follow the flumes carrying water for irrigation, up the hill just about as far as we could walk. These huge wooden flumes were square-cut wood, with side offshoots for watering the many rows of cane. They were big enough for a person to get down inside. Across the top of the flumes were slats for the workers to walk on and to observe the fields from above, and for maintenance. Sometimes the flumes went over gorges, but in this spot, most of the flume went straight downhill. The cane grew in fields of bright red dirt, out Haleiwa way. Caro and I would get down into the flume, all scrunched up, and would slide down the mountain, screaming like banshees. We'd get algae where people shouldn't get algae, and end up with green swimsuit or shorts bottoms. But it was fun, so of course we'd do it over and over again. I remember Mom's friend making us hose off outside and we had to eat our dinner outside, too. We were too messy to be allowed into her dining room. We had to sit on towels on the way home, but it was worth the scoldings. We loved those flume experiences and repeated them many times. I guess we were fortunate we never ran into cane field workers, or any of the overseers who would no doubt have told us that we were trespassing and to leave.

Elvis Presley was coming to town and giving a concert. Caro and I thought nothing of it. We'd seen Elvis on the Ed Sullivan show and thought he was cute, but there were other cute guys right at school! It soon became obvious that there WAS a groupie in our midst and that groupie happened to be Caro's mom. I can

Kapiolani Park aerial view, used under Creative Commons License 3.0: https://creativecommons.org/licenses/by/3.0/deed.en

still hear her gushing over how cute Elvis was, and "oh, those hips could go!" Our eyes would roll, and we'd nudge each other and laugh. Mom presented us with a handful of tickets to his show because *she needed to go with someone*. We and a couple of other girlfriends had the dubious pleasure of escorting Mom to and from the concert and were somewhat abashed at her tears and hysterics during the performance. We subsequently attended other concerts with Mom when he came back, and Mom remained the most devoted Elvis fan in Honolulu. Oddly enough, I got to meet Elvis at the Coco Palms Hotel on Kauai when he was there filming "Blue Hawaii." I wrote to Mom on the mainland where they'd moved, and she wrote back "Did you kiss him?" No, I didn't. Some people oohed and aahed, but I was too busy being cool. I was on my honeymoon.

Not all our experiences were fun. There was a graduation party we were invited to out on the north shore beach at Lanikai. We did have supervision in the house, and the food and company were great, with parents, grandparents and kids from the graduating class. When we went out around twilight in a group to go swimming, we found ourselves walking on hundreds of Portuguese man-of-war. A Portuguese man-of-war is a jellyfish-like, stinging hydrozoan. We all had wounds on our feet, and the parents ended up doctoring us up and applying vinegar. Some of us had swollen, painful feet for a few weeks. Equally as painful was the time I'd stepped on a sea urchin at Poipu Beach on Kauai. In that case, I had to wait for the spines to work themselves out of my foot.

I supposed there may have been some high school hanky-panky going on back then, but we were still at the innocent stage. We went out in groups, had fun in groups, and really didn't pair off until we were at least a couple years older. We were permitted to date at sixteen. My first real boyfriend played football and was two years ahead of me. Wow. I thought I was hot stuff. We broke up when he wanted me to marry him after he graduated. That was a "no-go," and I went on to date other guys.

Dad had a friend, Donny, who owned a restaurant on the north shore, and he gave us permission to use his cooking pit behind the restaurant. He'd stocked it with wood, started the fire, and opened his outside restroom for anyone who needed the facilities. Caro and her then-boyfriend Fred planned the party. Fred's best friend, Chuck, was a chef and in charge of the food on their ship, berthed at Pearl Harbor. Fred told us that Chuck would bring the food. Today, I'm sure that Uncle Sam paid for it, but back then, I didn't think anything of it, having known so many chefs who'd supplied the food for my parents' parties.

I remember juicy barbecue pork chops and chicken, corn on the cob, marshmallows and macaroni salad. I can still taste that food today. After we'd dowsed the fire, we kids all migrated across the street to the beach park, removed our sweatshirts and went swimming. We were young sailors, high school students, friends and relatives in a fairly large group. Events like this were commonplace. Someone always knew someone else, and before you knew it, you had an "event."

I've never had problems planning parties. Past experience helps and the main thing is deciding what to celebrate and whom to invite. After that, the planning seems to take care of itself. Our family Christmas parties are an example. I choose a weekend, then send the kids the date to show up at our home here on the Eastern Shore. The kids reserve that weekend. Some family members stay with us and some get hotel rooms in Ocean City. The kids and grandkids are encouraged to bring their friends.

For the Christmas holidays, I've always gone all out. Grandma reminded me as a child to do things well if I was going to do them at all, and to prepare early. If I'm making something for someone, I must treat it as an art project and make it as appealing as I can make it. I never got into trouble following Grandma's advice. I start working towards our annual Christmas party by the end of October. My very patient husband helps set up our huge tree in early November, helps with the lights, the garlands and the very tip-top, and I do the rest. It takes me up to a week to decorate our big Victorian tree and a smaller table tree with toys and candies for the kids (even though the youngest are now teens). I start with lights, glass or candy garlands, and layer out. Perhaps five hundred and more ornaments, poinsettia flower picks, and angels will fit on the large tree and perhaps seventy-five to a hundred cover the smaller table tree. Then I go on to decorate the house. In my free moments, I might finish a quilt for a family member or do some wrapping.

In the middle of the decorating process, there is always our community church Christmas bazaar. I'm fortunate that I love to bake, and they always let me bake and package the goodies with good sales in mind. I've become quite the marketer in my senior years. It's gratifying to earn so much money for the church (and yes, I've had fun)! After the church bazaar comes Thanksgiving, and we usually have a houseful; I enjoy opening the holiday season for the grandchildren who've come.

It's another excuse to make goodies.

My job is to cook and bake whatever the grandchildren (*mo'opunas*) ask for. I'm always happy when they start calling and telling me what they'd like to have me cook for them. Even if I haven't heard from them, I know what they like, and the food will be here waiting. I start baking and making desserts three or four days before the weekend. Two days before the gangs are due to arrive, I start on the main dishes—any number of casseroles, crab cakes and different seafood dishes, barbecue ribs and teriyaki steak, salads, maybe fruit bowls. There are always sirloin burgers and barbecue whiskey burgers on demand, or quesadillas. I do a lot of food prep so things can be made quickly on request. We usually have coolers and our extra refrigerator set up, and there is a bowl of punch and liquor set out. The extended family goes through a lot of food, but there are always lots of leftovers, especially desserts. I deliberately make a bunch extra, with care packages in mind. On the day my kids and their families pack up to leave, I pack up food and desserts for them to take home. Usually they have in-laws to visit, trips to take, and my kids have made their own Christmas traditions, but we always send them home with some of ours. After they leave, the house is always so quiet. Things don't begin to rev up again until December 26th, when I'm at it again, hitting the after-Christmas sales and buying half-price toys for the church's needy children for next Christmas. These toys are hidden under the beds in our house until next November when they will be delivered.

Recipes

Food. Food brings us together, hopefully in a good way. Every cook has a disaster to own—burned cookies, ingredient-measuring mishaps, and (horrors!) "healthy" ingredient substitutions resulting in culinary disaster. Becoming a good cook takes time, energy, and the will to make a dish someone actually wants to eat. Sometimes you get lucky and the recipe is perfect. Sometimes the result is less than beautiful, but tastes delicious. I'd say that practice makes perfect most times.

Don't be afraid to experiment with flavors. (However, don't experiment when you are feeding your mother-in-law or boss for the first time!) If you love blackened food, for example, experiment with your seasoning, particularly if you are sensitive to monosodium glutamate or Chinese food. There are several seasonings on the market, but most of the processed stuff has MSG. Find a good recipe on the internet and use the ingredients you like best. Some mixes are hot and others more savory. Don't be afraid to experiment until you find one you're happy with.

As the years have flown by and the family has grown larger, I've learned to take short cuts, using prepared foods or mixes as a starting point. For instance, one can make a moist pumpkin cake by adding a cup of canned pumpkin and some pumpkin pie spice to a yellow cake mix. If you're in a hurry (I usually am), prepared pie crusts are the way to go. Nowadays almost anything you want can be found on your grocer's shelves. To make a cake your own, use the mix, but make your frosting from scratch. Homemade frosting is so good, no one will notice or care that you may have used a cake mix. You can turn any frosting into a glaze by adding less sugar and keeping the mixture less stiff. Ugly cakes with messy frosting can be jazzed up with a sprinkling of nuts or rainbow jimmies.

We had a neighbor I adored. Roy was an excellent cook and baker, and every year he'd make us the most delicious Christmas cookies. At one of our parties I made an apple Bundt cake I thought he might enjoy. I followed the recipe faithfully, and the cake looked lovely on the cake dish. It smelled even better. All was well until Roy cut the first piece. My beautiful cake started to fall apart because the apples had been so juicy, the cake was too wet to set properly. So I went to the cabinet and pulled out some bowls, and we ended up having spoonsful of lumpy apple pudding. It was no less delicious, and as (everyone's) Grandma used to say, "If God gives you lemons, make lemonade." To this day, I don't know how that cake stood up so beautifully on the cake plate. It certainly gave us something to laugh about.

Classic recipes are great, but don't be afraid to improve on an old favorite. In the get-togethers of my childhood, *pupus* (appetizers) were frequently served while the teriyaki or fish was on the grill. We'd put chunks of ham and fresh pineapple with a little bit of cheese on toothpicks and serve them with a honey-mustard dip. We'd use mayo, honey, and mustard mixed well. This dip was also good on chunks of cooked chicken and on grilled shrimp. Later I changed the recipe a bit, changing the mustard to Dijon with horseradish and adding sriracha sauce for some bite. My husband loves this recipe, so I make it by the jar; it is excellent on chicken fingers and other meats. If you love fried onion rings, cheese sticks, french fries and zucchini sticks, this dip is a winner. (I can see my grandson, Sean, eating it with a spoon!)

If you are throwing a party or feeding a large group, do as much prep as you can beforehand. Making your casseroles and desserts ahead of time gives you more time with your guests, and all you have to do is to reheat. I often start my desserts—cookies, cakes, pies, candies—days before the event, sealed up and chilled; they'll keep. If I'm making whiskey barbecue burgers for my grandchildren, all the burgers can be made, bacon fried, potato salad mixed, and barbecue ribs or chicken precooked, ready for reheating and assembly.

If seafood is on the menu, you want fresh, so do those dishes the day before. If you don't have time to bake, buy melting chocolate, cookies off the shelf, and brownie bites from your grocer's bakery; dipped cookies and brownie bites make an impressive dessert. Drizzled chocolate over boxed caramel popcorn makes a good finger food. Dipping pretzels in melted chocolate makes a sweet–salty treat for those who want just a bite of something sweet. Go for it and experiment. If you are short on ideas, google it! The internet has been my inspiration for many of my own creations, and no doubt, it can be yours, too. Don't be afraid to use mixed vegetables in your soup recipes. Frozen vegetables are much "fresher" and better-tasting than canned vegetables. I detest cutting potatoes, so most frequently I buy frozen diced or hash brown potatoes. It sure beats nicks and scraped knuckles, and as long as the food tastes good, people don't care how your potatoes were cut. Shortcuts can be the difference between a successful or not so successful recipe. Baked potatoes are the exception to my "no fresh potatoes rule"—even then, I prick them with a fork and stick them in the microwave, bypassing the oven altogether. With all the butter, sour cream and dill, people love them, and the skins aren't too hard.

In short, be easy on yourself, and you can turn out some lovely dishes, focusing your time and energy strategically. People will appreciate the time you took to make them a lovely meal.

Here are some recipes that have brought some raves over the years. Hope you enjoy them.

Seafood Bake

For a variation, try adding a cup of shredded cheese to your seafood mixture before baking. This recipe is easy to add to, so make it your own with your favorite flavors. I've added chopped scallions and pimientos for color, extra shrimp, etc. It's easy to extend the recipe a bit by adding more mayo and breadcrumbs. Also, the recipe is very forgiving if an ingredient is forgotten, but a rule of thumb with crab meat is that mustard helps bring out the flavors, so don't forget that. I've found that regular yellow mustard is better with sweet barbecue sauces, while Dijon is suitable for seafood and fried food sauces. This rich recipe does well as an entrée for a simple dinner, accompanied by garlic bread and salad.

Ingredients:

- 1 pound picked cooked crab meat
- 1 pound cooked tiny shrimp
- 1 pound cooked baby scallops
- 1 1/2 cups mayonnaise
- 1 large egg, beaten
- **Seasonings and Condiments**:
    - 2 tablespoons fresh lemon juice
    - 1 tablespoon Worcestershire sauce
    - 1/2 teaspoon seafood seasoning
    - 1/2 teaspoon cayenne pepper
    - 1 teaspoon sriracha sauce, optional, but recommended
    - 2 tablespoons prepared Dijon mustard
- 1/2 cup panko or other dried breadcrumbs (divided)
- 2 ounces melted salted butter (1/2 stick)
- paprika

Directions:

1. Preheat the oven to 400 degrees. Spray a casserole pan with non-stick cooking spray.
2. Mix the cooked seafood and pour the mixture into the casserole dish.
3. In a separate bowl, mix mayonnaise, egg, seasonings and condiments. Stir in half of the breadcrumbs (1/4 cup).
4. Add the egg mixture to the seafood, mixing well and pressing the mixture flat. Top the casserole with the remaining breadcrumbs, drizzled butter, and a sprinkle of paprika.
5. Bake for 20 minutes, or until brown and bubbling.

Seafood Bake with Garlic Bread

Seafood Sauce

This sauce is delicious with crab cakes, baked and fried fish, or as a dip for steamed shrimp.

Ingredients:
- 1 1/2 cups mayonnaise
- 2 tablespoons capers, optional
- 2 tablespoons apple cider vinegar
- 2 tablespoons lemon juice
- 2 tablespoons Dijon mustard
- 2 tablespoons minced onion or 1 tablespoon onion powder
- 1 teaspoon sriracha sauce
- 1 teaspoon paprika

Directions:

Mix ingredients in a small bowl. Store leftovers in the refrigerator.

Crab or Shrimp Dip

You might want to make an extra dish of this to bring out later at your event. It goes quickly. I've used this dip as a sauce on top of blackened chicken fillets, and on blackened sword fish and mahi-mahi steaks. It's very savory and adds another layer of flavors to your entrée.

Ingredients:

- 1/2 pound picked, cooked crab meat or tiny cooked shrimp, drained well and patted dry. (If you have a crowd, double the recipe, using both crab meat and shrimp.)
- 8 ounces softened cream cheese

- 4 ounces sour cream
- 1–2 tablespoons sriracha sauce to taste
- 6 ounces shredded cheddar cheese-divided

Directions:

1. Preheat oven to 375 degrees and coat a small baking dish with non-stick cooking spray.
2. Blend sour cream and cream cheese together, then blend in the sriracha sauce.
3. Fold in the seafood and half of the shredded cheese, then place in the baking dish.
4. Top with the remaining cheese and bake until the cheeses have melted and dip is bubbly.
5. Serve with crackers, corn chips, or fried pita bread wedges.

Shrimp and Crab Dip on Crackers

Tartar Sauce and Tutu's Po' Boys

Phylis Okamoto taught me to make tartar sauce when I was knee-high to a grape. Phylis was the pie, cake and salad lady who worked at Fisherman's Wharf in Honolulu for years, and she taught me how to cook. (And she rented a cottage on our property on Kinau St. before we sold it.) This tartar sauce recipe was used at Fisherman's Wharf. We use this recipe on almost all our sandwiches, but it's especially terrific with shrimp po' boys and fish. My husband loves this sauce (and my po' boys) so I always keep it on hand.

I prefer to take the time and butter and grill my sandwich buns because doing so adds flavor and a crunchy texture to every bun for every type of sandwich. I also fry my Reubens and other sliced bread sandwiches. They are messy and gooey with melted cheese, sauce and fillings, but there is solution to sloppy sandwiches: waxed paper wrapped around the sides and bottom and peeling back the paper from the top as you go.

Tartar Sauce

What gives this tartar sauce its fresh flavor is the grated onion. The grating will give you that wonderful flavor without chunks of onion. This sauce is delicious on sandwiches, burgers, hot dogs, ham—anything with meat or poultry. I keep it in the fridge for just this purpose as well as for seafood. My hint here is to make a jar every time the mayo jar gets down to half full. (I typically use a 64-ounce jar of mayonnaise, but you may not need that much.) I mix the ingredients and store the tartar sauce in that jar. The tartar sauce doesn't last long enough in my house to spoil; my husband loves it on every sandwich he eats. I've also used the sauce as the dressing in seafood salad, with picked crab meat, sautéed and drained shrimp, chunked lobster, and chopped celery. This seafood salad, served on lettuce leaves with a sliced tomato gives you a good quick lunch. I also use the tartar sauce in tuna, ham, and bacon and egg salad (sometimes adding a little Dijon mustard for some kick.) Also, I add a little ketchup to it to make a rich Russian dressing for a decadent Reuben sandwich.

Ingredients:

- 32 ounces mayonnaise
- 1 onion, finely grated
- 1 cup sweet or dill pickle relish—I use the sweet.
- 1/3 cup chopped fresh or dried parsley
- 1 teaspoon lemon or lime juice to taste

Directions:

Mix all the ingredients together in the mayo jar or in a mixing bowl. Let the tartar sauce set for a few hours for the flavors to meld before serving. Keep refrigerated.

Po' Boy

Ingredients:

- Sandwich Rolls
- Butter
- Peeled and cleaned raw shrimp (enough to fill each sandwich roll, about 5 ounces per 6-inch roll)
- Cajun or Seafood seasoning
- Tartar sauce
- Shredded lettuce
- Sliced tomatoes

Directions:

1. Slice the sandwich rolls in half horizontally and hollow out the rolls by removing some of the bread from each half. Set aside.
2. Brown some butter in a hot pan, then add the shrimp. Season the shrimp with Cajun or seafood seasoning, and stir-fry until pink.
3. Layer lettuce, tomato, and tartar sauce in the base of the sandwich roll, and then pile the shrimp liberally on top. Finish the sandwich with the top half of the bun.
4. For a variation, toss seasoned shrimp with chopped onion, celery, and mayonnaise for a quick salad to fill your sandwich rolls or top a green salad

Shrimp Salad Po'Boy

Tutu's Dipping Sauce

I love this sauce for meats, seafood, and fried appetizers. This is another recipe where you can play with the amounts you use and adjust according to your family's tastes. I've used the sauce to stuff pita sandwiches on the fly. It's a wonderful alternative to plain mayonnaise.

Ingredients:

- 2 cups mayo
- 1/4 cup raw honey
- 1/4 cup Dijon mustard with horseradish
- 1 teaspoon sriracha sauce to taste
- 1 teaspoon paprika
- 1 teaspoon onion powder

Directions:

Mix ingredients in a small bowl. Serve with chicken fingers, chips, or other finger foods. Refrigerate leftover sauce.

Pita Stuffers

Use chicken or shrimp to make a salad that is delicious in a pita or in your favorite stuffed tomato recipe.

Ingredients:

- 2 cups cooked, diced chicken (leftover grilled chicken is great!) or clean, deveined, cooked shrimp, seasoned to taste
- 1 cup chopped celery

- 1/2 cup dried cranberries
- Tutu's Dipping Sauce, enough to bind ingredients

Directions:

1. Mix together protein, celery, and cranberries.
2. Toss in Dipping Sauce, mixing sufficiently to bind and coat ingredients.
3. Cut each pita in half, then split. Add the Pita Stuffer and your favorite sandwich toppers: lettuce, tomato, onions, olives, sweet and banana peppers.

Stuffed Flounder

You will need two fish fillets for each serving. If flounder is nowhere to be found, pollock or other white fish will make a delicious entrée.

Stuffing Ingredients:

- 1 stick butter (1/2 cup)
- 1 small onion, finely chopped
- 2 celery stalks, finely chopped
- 1 tablespoon fresh, chopped basil
- 1 tablespoon fresh, chopped parsley
- 1–2 cups chopped spinach leaves
- 1/2 cup finely chopped reconstituted sun-dried tomatoes
- 2 cups breadcrumbs (panko and Italian-seasoned are fine choices)

Stuffing Directions:

1. Melt a stick of butter in a small saucepan, and sauté the onions and celery. Add the basil and parsley and cook a minute or two until the onions are translucent.
2. Stir in the spinach and tomatoes, then add up to two cups of breadcrumbs.
3. Moisten the mixture with chicken broth just until the mixture is wet and the stuffing holds together.

Stuffed Fish Ingredients:

- Fish fillets—flounder or other white fish
- Olive oil
- Stuffing
- Lemon juice
- Seafood or Cajun seasoning
    Paprika

Stuffed Fish Directions:

1. Preheat oven to 350 degrees. Grease a baking pan.
2. Add one layer of fish to the baking pan.
3. Drizzle olive oil lightly over fish, then top fish with a thin layer of stuffing.
4. Place fish on top of the stuffing, pressing down slightly.
5. Drizzle fish with olive oil and lemon juice, and sprinkle fish liberally with your favorite seafood seasoning or Cajun mixture.
6. Bake until fish is flaky. Thicker fillets will take longer to cook, but you can start checking after 20 minutes.

This fish dish goes well with potato pancakes or fries, salad, and tartar sauce.

Stuffed Flounder

Chinese Barbecue Roast Chicken or Pork

Pork is traditionally used for this recipe, but chicken works well for those with religious restrictions.

Ingredients:

- 20-ounce jar of hoisin sauce
- 1 tablespoon minced garlic
- 1 tablespoon grated ginger
- 1/2 cup brown sugar

- Soy sauce to mix to light paste consistency
- 1–2 teaspoons star anise powder, optional
- 1 packet charsiu flavoring, optional. This is sold in Asian grocery stores or online. I buy it by the boxful.

Directions:

1. Mix all ingredients together and rub your bone-in or boneless chicken or white meats with the paste.
2. Let the meat sit and marinate for at least two or three hours in a gallon zip lock bag or big bowl, turning occasionally.
3. Preheat oven to 350 degrees. Roast meat on foil-lined pans: one hour for whole pieces and about 40 minutes for slices and flattened boneless thighs. Let sit five minutes before serving.

Chicken or Turkey Bake

This is a simple recipe and can feed as many people as needed. You can use chicken breast fillets, flattened boneless, skinless chicken thighs, sliced turkey cutlets or fillets, or any white meat, such as veal or pork. I've served this entrée with cranberry sauce and applesauce; either one complements the savory sage flavors.

Ingredients:

- Chicken or turkey fillets
- Garlic powder
- Poultry seasoning
- Finely chopped onions (about 1/3 cup for 6 fillets)
- Finely chopped celery (about 1/3 cup for 6 fillets)

- Dry stuffing mix
- Chicken or beef broth

Directions:

1. Preheat oven to 350 degrees.
2. In a greased pan, layer chicken or turkey fillets. Sprinkle fillets evenly with garlic and poultry seasoning.
3. Cover fillets evenly with onion and celery, then cover the fillets with a 3/4-inch layer of dry stuffing mix.
4. Top each fillet with some chicken or beef broth to moisten the stuffing layer, then add enough broth to the pan to just cover the meat (not the stuffing) while it bakes. (Beef broth deepens and enhances the flavors, but chicken broth works just fine, too.)
5. Cover the pan with foil and bake for about an hour at 350 degrees.
6. Let sit a few minutes before serving. Your chicken will be tender and juicy.

Hint: One of my favorite kitchen tips is to substitute some beef broth for chicken or turkey broth in soups and stews in order to deepen the flavors of the whole dish. I've made chicken soup and stews by cutting the chicken broth with beef, and everyone raves over it—by the time the dish is done, the broth has picked up the chicken flavoring and has enhanced the richness of the dish. Any bland meat will benefit from that infusion of flavor. **Caveat:** Chicken broth is better for seafood dishes.

Chicken Bake

Crab Cakes and Cocktail Sauce

I usually double the crab cake recipe, and we eat leftovers (if any) later. Crab cake sandwiches are so good! I've also served the fried crab cakes with scrambled eggs and sliced tomatoes for brunches. Some people like cocktail sauce with their crab cakes. I enjoy cocktail sauce once in a while, too, but not from a jar! Homemade is tastier, much fresher, and less bitter than store-bought.

Crab Cakes

Ingredients:

- 1 pound picked crab meat
- 1 large egg
- 1/2 cup mayonnaise
- 1 1/2 teaspoons dried mustard or 2 tablespoons prepared Dijon mustard
- 1 tablespoon Worcestershire sauce
- 1 teaspoon seafood seasoning
- 1/2 teaspoon white pepper
- 2 tablespoons chopped parsley
- 2 tablespoons minced green onions or chives
- 10–12 finely crumbled snack crackers

Directions:

1. Crumble crackers into a large bowl. Add the other ingredients except the crab meat, blend and let sit a few minutes to moisten the cracker crumbs. (You can use the time to double check your crab meat for pieces of shell or cartilage.)

2. Mix the crab meat into the mixture and form into round patties. I use my hands, but you can use an ice cream scoop.

Pan-fry: Heat about 1 1/2 inch of oil in a fry pan over a medium-high heat until the oil is 350 degrees. Fry cakes in hot oil until the cakes are brown, then flip them and cook for another minute or two. Drain on paper to soak up the grease prior to serving.

Bake: Preheat oven to 375 degrees. Lay the rounded cakes onto a well-greased lipped pan (like a jelly roll pan). Sprinkle with paprika and bake at 375 degrees for 15–20 minutes or until the crab cakes are firmly set and golden brown. Serve with seafood sauce or tartar sauce.

Crab Cakes and Seafood Sauce

Cocktail Sauce

This is excellent on all shrimp, and some people like it with broiled and fried scallops as well as crab cakes.

Ingredients

- 1 cup ketchup
- 2-4 teaspoons grated horseradish
- 1 tablespoon Worcestershire sauce
- 1-2 teaspoons lemon or lime juice to taste

Directions:

Put ketchup in a small mixing bowl. Add remaining ingredients one at a time to taste. Some people love horseradish (the more the better!) while others need something less severe. Cover and refrigerate sauce until needed.

Teriyaki

For the best flavor, begin the work for this recipe the day before your cookout so the meat can marinate overnight. When your fridge is full because you have the whole fam damily coming for July 4th weekend, forget the bowl: Throw the meat and marinade into gallon bags and tuck into an empty corner of the fridge. First, though, expel as much air as you can from the bags, seal the bag, then squish the meat around in the bag so the marinade touches all the meat surfaces.

Marinade Ingredients:

- 15-ounce bottle soy sauce (you may use low sodium)
- 1/2 cup brown sugar or more, to taste
- 1 tablespoon minced garlic
- 1 tablespoon grated ginger

Directions:

Mix ingredients together. Use as a marinade for meat of your choice.

Teriyaki Chicken Thighs with White Rice

Notes:

- Shrimp will need only an hour of soaking, while chicken and meats need up to half-day or overnight.

- You might want to roast your chicken on foil in the oven for about 40 minutes and finish it off on the grill outside over a charcoal fire. Most other meats can be done completely on the grill. Pull the lid down to prevent flareups. Charcoal provides the best flavor for teriyaki.
- After marinating the meats, throw away the leftover mixture. It should not be reused for marinating or as a dip for cooked meats.
- If you want to make Japanese-style skewered meat or chicken, soak the chunks or slices of meat first, and put on 'soaked' bamboo skewers right before getting them to the grill.
- Remember that poultry needs a little longer cooking time than meat does, and shrimp needs the least. As soon as shrimp are curled up on the skewer, they are done—sometimes as soon as one minute for each side, depending on the size of the shrimp. I try to buy the largest I can find.

Tutu's Fried Rice

Charsiu meats are the "go-to" for my fried rice, but shrimp is delicious, too. Cook the meats earlier, and chop finely to add to the fried rice. The fried rice is usually the last thing on the menu to cook because it takes such a short time to throw together, so have all your ingredients together at the onset.

Ingredients:

- 2 cups rice cooked with about 4 cups water till cooked, but still firm and not too mushy. Do not use instant rice, as it doesn't cook to the right consistency.
- Vegetable oil
- 4 large eggs, beaten

- 2 bunches green onions, clean and chopped
- 2 cups cooked meat, chopped
- Soy sauce
- Garlic powder

Directions:

1. Add about a tablespoon of oil to a hot pan. Pour in the beaten eggs and let them set. Turn the eggs over to finish cooking. Remove the eggs to a plate and shred them with a sharp knife.
2. Add more oil to pan and toss in the hot rice, stirring quickly.
3. Add the shredded eggs, chopped green onions, chopped cooked meat, chicken or shrimp.
4. Stir fry quickly for one or two minutes and drizzle with soy sauce. Sprinkle with a little garlic powder, and it's done. Do not overcook.

Notes:

- You may omit the meat and shrimp. Or add your favorite vegetables to the pot. Carrots and peas are often seen in Chinese restaurants, while broccoli and onions are never bad choices.

Slow Cooker Beef Soup with Onions

This is a rich, easy beef soup recipe, full of onions and flavor. We serve it sometimes on cold days with hot garlic bread.

Ingredients:

- 1 pound lean beefsteak (round or sirloin is fine)
- 2 quarts beef stock (I use the low-sodium variety)
- 3–4 onions, thinly sliced
- 1–2 sprigs thyme, or 1/2 teaspoon dried
- 4 cloves garlic, minced
- 1-pound bag frozen vegetables, optional
- 2 potatoes, diced, optional

Directions:

1. Place beef into a slow cooker, and add onions, thyme, and garlic.
2. Cover meat with broth and cook on low for at least three hours.
3. When beef is tender, take out and chop into small cubes and return to pot.
4. If you want a heartier soup, add frozen mixed vegetables and two diced potatoes. Simmer until veggies are tender, usually about a half hour longer.

The sky's the limit with this easy soup. Cooked rice or leftover noodles may be added to your soup, too. Just put them into your bowls and pour the hot soup over them. I've also made chicken soup in the slow cooker, leaving out the thyme, and later adding the frozen mixed vegetables. I usually use one box each of beef and chicken broths to enhance and deepen the chicken flavor. In the end, you will not taste the beef broth, and no one will guess that you've used it.

Slow Cooker Beef Soup with Garlic Bread

Italian Chicken Tortellini Soup

This is a rich, hearty Italian soup, which is excellent served with garlic bread. Sometimes I serve this soup with parmesan cheese or grated asiago on the side, to be sprinkled over the hot soup. Leftovers are delicious, and this recipe makes a lot of soup.

Ingredients:

- Olive oil, about 2 tablespoons
- 1 1/2 pounds ground chicken
- 6 cloves garlic, finely minced

- 1/2 teaspoon fennel seed
- 1 onion, chopped
- 2 quarts chicken broth, or 1 quart chicken broth plus one quart beef broth
- 1 can diced tomatoes, about 14 ounces
- 1 box baby portobello mushrooms (sometimes called crimini mushrooms), chopped
- 2 small zucchini, diced
- 1 teaspoon dried Italian seasoning
- 1 teaspoon dried basil
- 1 package refrigerated tortellini (about 20 ounces)

Directions:

1. Into a large soup pot (it'll need a lid), heat up two tablespoons olive oil, garlic, and fennel.
2. Add the ground chicken and cook until done.
3. Add onion, one quart broth, tomatoes, mushrooms, and zucchini, and simmer until vegetables are tender, perhaps an hour.
4. Stir in Italian seasoning, basil, and remaining broth. Bring to a simmer.
5. Add tortellini and cook about 10 minutes more.

I've used store-bought Italian sausage in this, or hamburger in place of ground chicken. If using something other than the chicken, leave out the fennel seed.

Note: When cooking with a lot of herbs in soups and stews, especially dried herbs, sometimes it's appropriate to put them in towards the end of the cooking process. The flavors are strong, and long cooking of some herbs makes them bitter. You want them to enhance your dish, not overpower it.

Tortellini Soup

Swiss Steak

I serve this entrée over rice or garlic-buttered noodles, and it's excellent.

Ingredients:

- 4-ounce pieces of the best quality steak you can afford. I use rib steaks or sirloin cut into pieces.
- Flour
- Garlic powder
- Salt and pepper
- Vegetable oil for frying
- 2 green or red bell peppers, chopped
- 1 onion, sliced
- 28-ounce can stewed or diced tomatoes, your preference

Directions:

1. Preheat oven to 350 degrees.

2. Use a meat pounder to pound the dry ingredients into a cut piece of steak.
3. Turn the meat over, apply the spices first, then apply flour, then pound again.
4. Repeat until meat is thin, just adding more flour at the end.
5. Set meat aside on waxed paper and repeat process for remaining pieces of meat.
6. Fry in hot oil until brown—meat will cook very quickly because of the thinness. (Meat will shrink while cooking).
7. Place the meat in a sprayed baking pan in a single layer. Add chopped peppers and sliced onions over each piece, then pour tomatoes over all.
8. Bake until the tomatoes are bubbly and flavors have blended, about 40 minutes.

Note: With a simple switch, this recipe can be the basis for a great country-fried steak dinner! Simply omit the veggies, drain the fat completely, and make a milk gravy, adding a little of the flour, garlic powder, salt and pepper for the traditional white gravy. Serve with corn bread or mac & cheese, whatever you want.

Swiss Steak over Rice

Japanese Stir Fry with Tofu

For stir fries, begin with a hot pan and a little heated oil before adding ingredients. A wok works great, but it's not necessary. Stir fries cook quickly because the pan is preheated, so prepare your meats and vegetables first. Begin cooking tough veggie pieces a couple minutes before adding the tender veggies. Fish will fall apart in a stir fry, but shrimp holds up well.

Beef Stir Fry with Tofu

Ingredients

- 1 package firm tofu, cubed
- 1–2 cups watercress
- 1 bunch green onions, cleaned and sliced
- Fresh or canned vegetables such as bean sprouts, bok choy, carrots, broccoli, onions, and bell peppers
- Shrimp (4 ounces per serving) or boneless meat: beef, chicken, or pork (3 ounces per serving)
- 1–2 ounces vegetable oil
- Minced garlic to taste (powder is fine in a pinch)

(*continued*)

- Grated ginger (powder works well, too)
- 2–4 tablespoons brown sugar to taste
- 1–2 ounces soy sauce (low sodium is fine)

Stir Fry Veggies with Chicken

Directions

1. Remove tofu from its package and liquid, and slice into 3/4-inch cubes. Set aside.
2. Clean watercress, chopping off roots and removing thick, tough stems. Set aside.
3. Clean and slice green onions. Set aside.
4. Prepare vegetables of your choice by washing, drying, draining, or slicing: julienne carrots; drain canned vegetables; cut bok choy, broccoli, bell peppers and yellow onions into bite-sized pieces. Plan to cook "tougher"

vegetables longer by adding them to the pan before adding the more tender vegetables. Set aside.
5. Prepare shrimp by deveining and peeling. (A shrimp tool will do this effectively in a single motion.) Prepare meat by slicing it thinly so it will cook quickly.
6. Heat up a small amount of oil in a wok or frypan.
7. Into the hot pan, add the meat pieces or shrimp, turning them often.
8. Add the garlic and ginger.
9. When the meat is mostly cooked, stir in a little brown sugar and one or two splashes of soy sauce, continuing to turn the meat.
10. Add the tough vegetables, then tofu, watercress, green onions, and other vegetables, continuing to turn the mixture until the meat and vegetables are cooked and heated through.
11. Serve stir fry over steamed rice.

Variation with Soba Noodles

For a variation on your stir fry, try tossing in some prepared soba noodles from your neighborhood Asian store, adding in a bit of siracha and a little more brown sugar for a "sweet-hot" taste. Soba noodles are sticky because of the starch. After cooking, if there are extra, toss them in a bowl with a tablespoon or two of canola or vegetable oil, and seal them up in a Ziploc bag—they will keep for a few days. I don't know if they freeze well because they've never lasted that long in our home.

Easy Tex-Mex Night at Tutu's

For quick meals, I often rely on a few Tex-Mex staples. The grandchildren are always hungry, and these are easy to make. I almost always have a rotisserie chicken or a bowl of taco beef in the fridge, along with tortillas, chips, cheese, canned refried beans and toppings. These ingredients can be used to make nachos, quesadillas, burritos, and enchiladas. If you like spicy food, you can also stock cans of jalapeno peppers and keep a jar of chili pepper flakes on hand.

Quesadillas

Ingredients:

You may use any ingredients that you like, but this list lends itself to a multitude of quick recipes:

- Rotisserie chicken
- Taco beef
- Grated cheddar or Mexican three-cheese mix

(*continued*)

- Sour cream
- Individual packs of guacamole
- Black olives, canned
- Tortillas
- Corn chips
- Tortilla chips
- Whole kernel corn, canned
- Refried beans, canned
- Jalapenos, sliced fresh or canned
- Tomatoes, chopped
- Lettuce, chopped
- Onions, chopped
- Enchilada sauce, jar
- Salsa, jar
- Queso cheese dip
- Taco Seasoning
- Garlic
- Cumin
- Chili Pepper flakes

Taco Beef

Directions:

1. In a little olive oil, fry up two or three pounds of lean ground beef. Add a tablespoon of minced garlic and a chopped medium onion for each pound of beef.
2. Drain the excess grease from your cooked beef, stirring in 2-3 packets of taco seasoning.
3. Add a half cup of water, and cook together a minute or two.
4. Store in a covered bowl or zip lock bag. This recipe can be frozen and stored in a freezer bag until needed.

Taco Chicken

The easy way to make taco chicken is to use a rotisserie chicken from the grocery store. This recipe requires quite a bit of taco seasoning—about 4 ounces per chicken.

Directions:

1. Pick the meat from the bones of a rotisserie chicken, shredding the meat. Set aside.

2. Sauté a chopped onion in a little olive oil, add the chicken, 4 ounces of taco seasoning, and a small amount of water. Cook together a few minutes.
3. For a variation, cook some boneless skinless chicken thighs in a covered pan, with a chopped onion, a couple of cloves of minced garlic, 2-4 ounces of taco seasoning. Add water if the chicken does not produce enough liquid when cooking.
4. Freezer bags come in handy for keeping the chicken fresh. Chicken can be stored in the freezer until needed.

Nachos

Directions:

1. Place corn or tortilla chips in a microwave-safe dish.
2. Add spoonsful of the taco beef, chile, or chicken.
3. Top the chips with other ingredients of your choosing: refried beans, black olives, jalapenos, for example.
4. Add a generous amount of grated cheddar or Mexican three-cheese mix and microwave until the cheeses have melted and the dish is hot.
5. Top with your choices of chopped tomatoes, lettuce, and onions, and serve with salsa, guacamole and sour cream.
6. For a variation, heat nacho cheese dip and pour over the nachos in place of grated cheese.

Quesadillas

Directions:

1. Spread out one or more large tortillas on a clean surface.
2. On half of each tortilla, lay refried beans, taco beef or chicken, chopped olives (optional) and a generous amount of grated cheese. Fold the empty side of the tortilla onto the covered side. Press each tortilla as flat as possible, keeping the fillings from spilling out.
3. Heat a frying pan with a pat of butter until sizzling.

4. Using a big spatula, carefully place a folded tortilla on one side of the pan, with the fold in the center of the pan.
5. Grill until a luscious golden brown, then flip, keeping the folded side in the center of the pan. This keeps the fillings from escaping.
6. Carefully remove to a large plate and cut into two or three sections with a pizza cutter wheel. Nuke for a min. to heat through and serve with salsa, guacamole and sour cream.

Tex-Mex Bacon Relish

This ingredient for Tex-Mex dishes is optional. I often make a Mesquite bacon onion relish to add flavor to several dishes. This recipe requires bacon, onions, and mesquite or chipotle seasoning.

Directions:

1. Chop up a pound of turkey or regular bacon and two onions.
2. Cook and drain bacon.
3. Add the onions, mesquite or chipotle seasoning, and some garlic to the pan, and sauté until the onions are cooked.

Easy Burrito Rollups

Directions:

1. Lay out a tortilla on a sheet of waxed paper.
2. Center right place a few tablespoons of refried beans, taco meat or chicken, a tablespoon of salsa, and grated cheese. Fold tortilla three times to roll the burrito: right-to-left, bottom-up (like a diaper), left-to-right. Fold the waxed paper over the rolled tortilla the same way, securing the covered tortilla with a tooth pick.

3. Microwave the wrapped burrito on a plate for a minute or two until heated through and cheese has melted.
4. Serve with salsa, sour cream and guacamole.

Enchilada Bake

Any number of ingredients can be used in this recipe—add your family's favorites!

Directions:

1. Preheat oven to 350 degrees.
2. Spray a large casserole dish with non-stick spray.
3. Take a corn or flour tortilla and layer your choices of refried beans, meat, olives, corn, Spanish rice, and little enchilada sauce and cheese. Roll tortilla and place in pan, open side down. These can be messy, so don't over fill.
4. Repeat the tortilla rolls until casserole dish is full. Pour enchilada sauce over the layer of enchiladas and add a good sprinkle of the grated cheese. You may add another layer if needed, with another can of sauce and more cheese.
5. Bake at 350 degrees for a half hour or until cheeses have melted and dish is sizzling. (Sometimes if I'm out of the sauce, I pour a can of stewed diced tomatoes over the enchilada with the cheese...still a delicious casserole dish.)

Taco Casserole

Directions:

1. Preheat oven to 350 degrees.
2. Spray a large casserole dish with non-stick spray.
3. Layer broken corn chips, taco meat or chicken, refried or canned beans, corn, rice, olives, enchilada sauce, or diced tomatoes in juice, and cheese. Repeat layers of your choice,

leaving room for casserole toppings. The corn chips at the bottom will absorb moisture from the other ingredients and make a cohesive casserole.
4. On top of the casserole, add another can of enchilada sauce, crumbled corn chips, and grated cheddar.
5. Bake casserole until bubbling, about 45-60 minutes. A convection oven will take less time to cook. Serve with guacamole and sour cream.

Enchilada Bake

Easy Chinese Spareribs

Sweet-and-sour pork spareribs are a staple of Cantonese meals in Hawaii. They are simple to prepare; use the sauce of your choice. I use my own sweet-and-sour barbecue sauce or General Tso's bottled sauce for serving. For those who don't eat pork, beef short ribs create spectacular results. (In our house, that means there are no leftovers.) I've also used the vinegar/brown sugar method described here for cooking chicken wings, and they take much less time to cook—perhaps 30–45 minutes with a light simmer. I cut off the tips first, and then just cook the whole wing.

Ingredients:

- Beef short ribs or pork spareribs
- Sweet-and-sour Barbecue Sauce (below)
- 2-3 cups apple cider vinegar
- 6 tablespoons minced garlic
- 6 tablespoons grated ginger
- 1 cup light brown sugar

Directions:

1. Cut ribs into segments and place in pot.
2. Cover ribs with apple cider vinegar, minced garlic, and grated ginger. Add brown sugar and water enough to cover the ribs.
3. Cover the pot tightly with a lid and simmer until the meat starts to fall off the bone. (Or cook in your slow cooker.)
4. When the meat is tender, pour the contents of the pot into a large colander to drain off the liquid. Discard the bones that have separated from the meat, then pour the drained meat into a large bowl.
5. Add the sauce to the meat and toss.

6. Serve ribs and sauce with rice or complementary Chinese dishes.

Sweet & Sour BBQ Spareribs

Sweet-and-Sour Barbecue Sauce

This is a forgiving and versatile recipe. I've used honey in place of brown sugar and added other ingredients like chili sauce and flaked chili peppers. I have made it so often that I never measure anything anymore. If I think it's too thick, I'll add a little extra vinegar, but we like thick sauce, so I don't usually add water. If the sauce is running low and I'm hosting a cookout, I have been known to add commercial barbecue sauce to stretch out what I have. It's always good! The essence of the homemade sauce remains, and the commercial sauce simply enhances the flavors. Experiment and see what appeals to you. Delicious on rice.

Ingredients:

- 1 stick butter
- 2 medium onions, finely chopped
- 1 warehouse-size bottle ketchup (about 114 ounces)
- 3/4 cup apple cider vinegar
- 4 ounces liquid smoke
- 1 cup brown sugar, to taste
- 4 tablespoons prepared mustard
- 4 tablespoons Worcestershire sauce

Directions:

This sauce is good on ribs, chicken, fish and shrimp. Roast, bake or grill the meat, poultry, or seafood, using your favorite seasonings. When the meat is cooked through, apply sauce and continue cooking for an additional ten minutes. If you cook your meat on bamboo skewers, soak the skewers first for several hours so they won't burn. With food on the grill, leave the lid lowered to minimize flare-ups, and don't top the meat with the sauce too soon to avoid burning the sugar in the sauce.

Appetizers: For appetizers, add cooked meatballs to the sauce, or pour sauce over chunks of cooked chicken or meat, and offer toothpicks and napkins. They never last too long.

Sandwiches: This sauce is great for making barbecue for pulled chicken, pork or beef sandwiches. Prepare the poultry and meat by wet-cooking with liquid smoke. After pulling and shredding the cooked meat, toss in the barbecue sauce to your desired taste.

Barbeque Chicken, Fried Rice, and Broccoli

Streusel Love

Have your streusel topping made. I keep bags of it in the fridge for quick desserts, especially during the summer, when peaches and blueberries are wonderful. Streusel is usually made with butter, flour, brown and white sugars, cinnamon, and sometimes various nuts and coconut. I keep gallon bags of streusel in the fridge...After the butter, sugars and flour, I add cinnamon, toasted macadamia nuts and coconut to mine.

Ingredients

- 1 cup butter, softened (2 sticks)
- 1 cup flour
- 2 cups brown sugar
- 1 cup white sugar
- 3 tablespoons cinnamon
- 2 cups roasted macadamia nuts, chopped
- 14-ounce bag sweetened flaked coconut

Streusel Topping

Directions

1. Add butter, flour, sugars, and cinnamon to a large mixing bowl. Blend ingredients together well with pastry blender.
2. Add the macadamia nuts and coconut to the mixture, blending by hand to eliminate clumps.
3. Store unused portion in the refrigerator.

Fruit Streusel

Slice 6-8 peaches or cooking apples into a greased baking dish and mix a cup or two of the streusel with the fruit, adding a few squeezes of lemon juice. Top mixture with two or three cups of the streusel. Bake at 350 degrees until bubbly, or in the case of apples, until tender. (I slice apples quite thinly.) During the summer, we always keep French vanilla ice cream in the freezer for these quickly baked desserts.

Peach Streusel

My favorite hint is to not be afraid to use box mixes. I use them as a base when I'm in a hurry, and make them my own, with some experimentation. No one has ever asked me, "Is this a mix?" The results are too ono. Delicious.

Quick Peach Streusel Cake

Follow a yellow cake mix recipe according to instructions, except: Use 1 1/4 cups peach puree instead of water. (Add eggs and butter or oil according to the box directions.) After pouring batter into a greased and floured rectangular cake pan, top the batter with a liberal amount of streusel. Bake until a toothpick comes out clean and cake is firm. After the cake cools slightly, pour **Cream Cheese Glaze** (below) over the whole top of the cake, then let it sit and cool a bit before serving.

Quick Orange Streusel Cake

This recipe calls for a box of yellow cake mix as well. In the wintertime when fresh fruits are not as plentiful, I've substituted a 15-ounce can of mandarin oranges, minus half the juice, for the liquid in the cake mix. (Add eggs and butter or oil according to the box directions.) The oranges come apart easily with an electric beater and make a delicious orange cake, with or without the streusel topping. Sometimes I add a few drops of orange extract and some freshly grated orange zest to deepen the flavors. To the **Cream Cheese Glaze** (below), I add a little fresh orange juice (a tablespoon or two), and orange zest before pouring over the warm cake.

Orange Streusel Cake

Blueberry Coffee Cake with Streusel and Cream Cheese Glaze

This coffee cake makes for a delicious breakfast or snack. Experiment with other berries, whatever is fresh and in season at your local grocer or farmers market.

Cake ingredients:

- 3 cups of self-rising flour
- 1 cup sugar
- 3/4 cup sour cream
- 3 eggs
- 4 ounces melted butter (1 stick)
- 1 teaspoon vanilla
- 1/4–1/3 cup whipping cream   (*continued*)

- 1 pint blueberries
- Streusel topping

Directions:

1. Preheat oven to 350 degrees.
2. In large bowl, stir self-rising flour and sugar until well mixed.
3. Add sour cream, eggs, butter, vanilla, and whipping cream. (Whipping cream makes a thicker batter.) Beat until just smooth. Batter is usually stiff. Remember, if you add too much cream, your coffee cake will take longer to bake.
4. Stir in blueberries.
5. Pour mixture into a greased 9"X13" baking pan, and cover with streusel.
6. Bake at 350 degrees for 40–50 minutes, until a straw or toothpick comes out cleanly.
7. While still very warm, glaze with Cream Cheese Glaze.

Blueberry Coffee Cake

Cream Cheese Glaze

Ingredients

- 8 ounces cream cheese (1 box)
- 4 ounces butter (1 stick)
- 2 1/2 cups confectioners' sugar
- 1 teaspoon vanilla

Directions

1. Microwave cream cheese and butter for about a minute until butter is almost melted and cream cheese is soft.
2. Add confectioners' sugar and vanilla and beat with a mixer until smooth.
3. Pour glaze over warm cake. Let sit until very cool before cutting, (although my husband cannot wait and usually digs in before the glaze has set)!

Triple Fudge Brownies

These brownies are dedicated to extreme chocolate lovers. What puts these brownies over the top is chocolate-cream-cheese icing.

Triple Fudge Brownies

Ingredients:

- 3 sticks butter, melted (1 ½ cups)
- 3 cups sugar
- 2 tablespoons vanilla
- 5 large eggs
- 2 cups flour
- 1 teaspoon baking powder
- 1 teaspoon salt
- 1 cup cocoa powder
- 12-ounce package chocolate chips

Directions:
1. Preheat oven to 350 degrees. Grease and flour a 9" x 13" baking pan.
2. In a large mixing bowl, beat melted butter, sugar, and vanilla until mixed well.
3. Add one egg to mixture, beating it into the mixture until creamy. Add and beat in the remaining eggs, one at a time.
4. Add dry (powder) ingredients and stir until mixed well.
5. Fold in chocolate chips.
6. Pour batter into the baking pan and bake for one hour.
7. Test for doneness by inserting a toothpick into the center of the brownies. When the brownies are done, the toothpick will come out clean.

These brownies are very dense and rich. They can be dusted with cocoa powder or frosted with this:

Chocolate Cream Cheese Frosting

This icing is simple to make and so rich! Use it in place of "ordinary" chocolate frosting on your next cake or batch of brownies.

Ingredients:

- 1 stick soft butter (1/2 cup)
- 8 ounces cream cheese, softened
- 3/4 cup cocoa powder
- 1 pound confectioner's sugar
- 2 tablespoons vanilla
- Whipping cream, optional

Directions:

1. With a mixer, beat butter and cream cheese until light and fluffy.
2. Add dry ingredients and vanilla and beat well.
3. Whipping cream (1–3 ounces) may be added to the mixture for a creamier consistency.

Triple Fudge Brownies with Chocolate-Cream Cheese Frosting

French Cream

This delicious pudding can be used for so many recipes, including cream pies, cream puffs, and trifle. For this recipe, you'll need a heavy pot and a whisk.

Ingredients:

- 6 large eggs
- 1 cup flour
- 1 1/2 cups sugar
- 1 scant teaspoon salt
- 3 12-ounce cans evaporated milk, with water (about 1 1/2 cups) added to make 6 cups liquid total
- 1/2 stick COLD butter
- 4 teaspoons real vanilla extract

Directions:

1. Slightly beat the eggs in a small-to-medium mixing bowl. Set aside.
2. Whisk dry ingredients in the pot until well blended.
3. Add the diluted milk to the pot, stirring well, making sure there are no lumps. Cook over a medium heat stirring and scraping the bottom of the pan constantly for 6–7 minutes until thick and bubbling.
4. Add a portion of the flour and milk mixture into the eggs and whisk briskly. Turn the egg and flour mixture into the pot, continuing to whisk briskly. This tempering prevents the eggs from cooking too quickly. Continue to cook and whisk 2–3 minutes longer. The mixture should be bubbling gently and very thick.
5. Remove the pot from the heat. Add the cold butter and vanilla, whisking them in as the butter melts. The butter and

vanilla added at the end adds glossiness to the pudding and the vanilla adds the underlying flavor.

This pudding can be cooled and used, as is, to fill cream puff and eclair shells and for pudding layers in trifle bowls. It is also delicious with freshly sugared fruit, such as strawberries and peaches in dessert bowls.

Cream Pies

French Cream can be adapted for numerous cream pie recipes. This recipe will make two pies and a little extra pudding, or you may skimp a bit and eke out three pies, particularly in recipes where the pudding is sharing a pie shell with other ingredients.

Pie Crusts: You may use any pie crust, homemade or off-the-shelf, but I usually use store-bought 9-inch graham cracker or cookie crusts from the baking aisle of the grocery store. To prepare those, I brush them with an egg and water mixture and bake them at 350 degrees for 5–6 minutes. This way, they'll be leak-proof and don't crumble when the pies are cut. There are a variety of cookie crust flavors on store shelves now, like chocolate, graham cracker and cookie. Generally, I think the cookie pie crusts that are commercially available are worthy complements to the cream fillings. (And they take less time to prepare!) Experiment and decide what you like in your pie combinations.

Pie Topping: I usually use a tub of non-dairy whipped topping for topping cream pies; this topping keeps its shape pretty well and doesn't "melt" as quickly as real whipped cream. However, real whipped cream is a lovely choice when the whole-pie presentation is not important. In that case, add the whipped cream just before serving.

Banana Cream Pie

Spoon about a cup of warm filling into your favorite prepared pie crusts. Layer slices of ripe bananas (about 2 bananas) over the filling and top with more filling. Repeat, if desired. The warm filling draws out the flavors of the fruit. The bananas will not discolor, but they must be ripe. Let cool and chill for a couple of hours before topping with whipped topping.

Pina Colada Cream Pie

Spread half of a 21-ounce can of pineapple pie filling into the bottom of each pie shell, then top with the coconut filling. After cooling, top with whipped topping and garnish with flaked coconut.

Maple Pecan Pie

If you are looking for a taste of fall any time of the year, make maple pecan pies. Add about one tablespoon of maple extract (to taste) to the warm pudding, as well as 1 1/2 cups of chopped, lightly toasted pecans. This filling is good in graham cracker crusts. It is also delicious spooned onto squares of fresh gingerbread or apple cake.

Chocolate Cream Pie

Add one package of your favorite chocolate chips (about 12 ounces) to the hot pudding. Stir the pudding until the chips have melted. Divide the mixture between two baked pie shells, chill and top with whipped topping. Garnish with a shaved chocolate bar.

Chocolate Cream Pie

Coconut Cream Pie

Add one tablespoon of coconut extract and one 7-ounce bag of sweetened coconut flakes to the hot pudding. Pour the filling into your shells, chill, and top with whipped topping. Garnish with flaked coconut.

Trifle

A trifle is a wonderful dessert that features any variety and combination of ingredients—fruits, pudding, cake, whipped topping, chocolate. Layered colorfully into a glass bowl, a trifle is a beautiful finish at any family gathering, or a delicious and attractive addition to the dessert table at your next community fundraiser. This recipe assumes French Cream as the pudding component of the trifle, but feel free to use any pudding that you like!

Directions:

Into a clear glass trifle bowl, layer your cake, pudding, fruits, whipped topping, up to the top of the dish, and then garnish. Make sure each layer goes to the edge of the bowl for a beautiful presentation.

Note: A trifle bowl is a large, clear, deep glass bowl with straight sides and a pedestal that is conducive to layering dessert or salad ingredients deliberately. There are also mini trifle bowls on the market for individual serving, too. Don't feel like you must go out and buy a special trifle bowl! Trifle is delicious however it is assembled.

For **Strawberry Trifle**, you might layer squares of lemon cake, pudding, strawberries, and whipped topping.

For **Chocolate Cookie Trifle**, you can layer broken sandwich cookies, Chocolate French Cream Pie filling, and whipped topping. Garnish with broken cookies over the whipped topping.

At our parties, the Chocolate Cookie Trifle is always the first to go. For the 4th of July, I've made a "red-white-and-blue" **Old Glory Trifle** with fresh strawberries and blueberries, strawberry and/or blueberry pie filling, yellow cake cubes, French Cream and whipped topping. (This is my favorite of the trifles, but my husband and grandkids go for the chocolate.)

Chocolate Cookie Trifle

Tutu Pa's Tales from the Taro Patch

by C.M. "Muzzy" Marcallino

My dad loved everything about Hawaiian culture, and among the things was the local language. He enjoyed telling tales on his radio show, and he came up with some wonderful original content. Enjoy these poems adapted from Western children's story classics. They are meant to be read aloud and require some practice. Don't omit the swagger! My dad was one of a kind.

Da Ehu Kumu in Her Red Muumuu

    Wunce upon won forest place
        A ole grammama stay
    Sick insigh da punee bed
      So no can run an play.

    But luky ting she get gran keed
        One girl wit luau feet[5]
    An evry time dis girl stay breeng
        Good stuffs for Tutu eat.

    One day dis gal stay stahting out
        Wit her puka lauhala[6] baskit

---

[5] big feet [slang]
[6] pandamus

She treeping true da forres trale
    Stay seenging tisket – tasket.

She waring on red muumuu[7]
    An red ridin' hoods to boot
But her Li'o (hoss) went mak'e[8]
    So she gotta walkeen foots.

One big bad woluff wit spy glass
    He stay spock dis lass a kummin
From da pali[9] top, he sheeft his geahs
    An full speed kum a runnin.

This woluff was smaht cause he went skool
    He's a kool kat, smaht at talkin
So he wags his tale and he say "Aloha!"
    Wen "Red" she kums by walkin.

Wen he spock dat lassy wit da melly chassy
    About dat tendah stuffs he's dreemin
So he leek his leeps an he doffs his hat
    An heez branes stahteen to skeeming.

"Whea-you-stay-go an what you got?"
    The wolfie axk ouah Red
"I get kaukau[10] an okolehao[11]
    For feed Tutu,"[12] she said.

"A, whea she live? Get lock da doah?"
    Da beeg bad woluff say

---

[7] women's slip, gown
[8] her horse died
[9] cliff
[10] food
[11] liquor made from ti root
[12] grandmother

An wen pooah Red she tells him dat
    Da woolfie runned away.

Firs he check up da map, den he speen his wheel
    To da pooah grammama's howse
He deesgize his woice like wun leedle girl
    An he fool Tutu... Dat louse!

He streep off her clodes an he tie her up
    Stuff some rag eensigh her face
Den he trow her een da klozzet
    An he lox her een dat place.

He ware on hur clodes, jump eesigh da bed
    'Til da porky Red she kum
An wen she noxxing on da dooah
    Da smaht woluff, he play dumb.

"Com een," he said, "I'm seek da bed!"
    He meemick Tutu's woice
"Yu breeng kaukau?[13] I'ze hunngah now
    for fude I stay rejoice!"

Red kum eensigh grammama's hale[14]
    Hur baskit open wide
"What get? What get?" da woluff sez
    "What goodies get eenside?"

"Get fat laulau[15] an poi,"[16] she tell,
    "An polokee sudeesh[17]
An one sak'e jug an boddle oke

---

[13] food
[14] house
[15] steamed, stuffed ti leaves
[16] boiled and pounded taro root
[17] Portuguese sausage

      an sum poki[18] aku[19] feesh."

"But grammama, how beeg youah eye"
      Ouah luvahly gurlie said.
"How good for spock youah figger up
      From luau feets to head."

"An oh! Dat nose! How fat an long,
      I nevvah seed like dat!"
"Moah bettah for whiffum," da woluff tell
      Dat onolishus[20] brat.

"An doze beeg white teets, how long an sharp,"
      Da lovahly ladee say.
"Da bettah for suckum you body up,
      An chu you, hips hoooray!"

Wit dat, da woluff jumps out da bed
      Da spocks shine frum heez eye
An skreems for hellup kum from her throte
      An dere hurd on Molokai.

Den da cockeye mayah een hiz coconut hat
      Wit a swift kum down da pali
An he stop da beet of his lio's[21] feet
      At dah pooah grammama's hale.[22]

He reeds hiz skript, lifts da hosses tail
      An he hemo[23] one green panini[24]

---

[18] sliced or cubed
[19] skipjack tuna
[20] ono = good, onolishus = good delicious
[21] horse's
[22] house
[23] remove, take off
[24] cactus fruit

Wheech he jams two feet up da woolfie's butt
    Coz da mayah, he ain't manini.[25]

Da woluff he howl an da woluff he moan
    An he spleet for Kaleponi[26]
An dey saves Tutu, den dey marry up
    An dats no dam baloney.

So dis ees da en to dat legen taail
    But befoah I go holoholo[27]
Ouah Red an da mayah lived forever happily
    Puffin' dere paka lolo.[28]

---

[25] reticent [slang]
[26] California
[27] wander off, take off
[28] literally, crazy tobacco, marijuana

Da Nite Befoa Kalikamaka

Twas da nite befoa Kalikamaka[29] an all thru' da hale[30]
Not one ting stay moving, not even iole.[31]

Da eke[32] stay hang on da hao[33] bush wit care
We stay hope St. Nikolaka soon kum o'dere.

Da keikis[34] stay moi-moi[35], dey stay cool off dere head
Dey stay look-see papayas, stay spin round in dere heads.

An I get me new malo[36], Mama get new muumuu[37], oh boy!
We eat up fish and poi, now we go hea-moi[38].

When outside in the loi[39], oooh! we hear da kine swearings
We jump outside from da punee[40] for look see "who burn bearings."

Den we leeps to da window, yea, we fly like a swift
Da garbage outside sure been let off one whiff.

Da mahina[41] was shined like da day on da land

---

[29] Christmas
[30] house
[31] mouse
[32] bag
[33] lowland tree
[34] children
[35] hushed
[36] loin cloth
[37] women's dress
[38] fall asleep
[39] irrigated taro fields
[40] couch
[41] moon

An Hawaii 's fair beauties went reflect from the sand.

When what to our maka,[42] and don't tink we're looney
We spark one canoe and get eight menehune.[43]

And dere in da loi, wit mud to his knees
He stay hemo[44] red pants but he get red BVDs.

Was one jolly old steersman, so swift and so quick
We knowed in one second dat it was St. Nick.

Da menehunes grab up da oars, tru' da loi dey came
And he whistle and shout an he call dem by name.

"Hoe[45] Moke, hoe Loke, hoe Masa and Dixie
Hoe Ah-Tong and Sul-An, hoe José and Trixie."

"To da top of da kamani[46] tree, to da top of da wall
Now hoe away, hoe away, hoe away all!"

More dry den da lau, da makani[47] make fly
As dey huli and twist and fly high in da sky.

To da top of da hale, da menehune dey flew
Wit da canoe full with toys and St. Nickolaka[48] too.

An den from da roof we can hear ukulele
Menehunes stay singing all da-kine Xmas meles.[49]

---

[42] eye, eyesight
[43] little men, Hawaii's elves
[44] remove, take off
[45] paddle, as a canoe
[46] shoreline tree
[47] wind, winds
[48] Nicholas
[49] songs, chants

Den we pull in our po'o⁵⁰ an rubber-neck around
And we look ole St. Nick, he jump in wit a bound.

In dose red BVDs and one malo⁵¹ and boots
He stay dress all in red from papale⁵² to foots.

An one big eki⁵³ toys, stay hapai⁵⁴ on his back
An he look so goofy, we stay laugh, dat's a fack.

His maka,⁵⁵ dey sparkles, his voice was how merry
Like a wino his face and his nose like a cherry.

His teeth stay nihoole,⁵⁶ an we say, cause we know
Dat his umi-umi⁵⁷ was akeokeo⁵⁸ like da Mauna Kea snow.

An stuck in his mug was one Toscani cigar
You could smell he was coming from near and from far.

His mouth it stay smiles, he get nui-nui opu⁵⁹
And it shake when he laugh like one bowl full pupu.⁶⁰

Ole St. Nick was momona,⁶¹ he was round like one ball
An me an my Mrs., ooooh, we laugh til we fall.

---

⁵⁰ head
⁵¹ loin cloth
⁵² hat
⁵³ bag
⁵⁴ carry
⁵⁵ eyes
⁵⁶ missing
⁵⁷ beard
⁵⁸ snow
⁵⁹ big stomach
⁶⁰ hors d'oevres
⁶¹ fat

But he wink two-side maka,[62] den he twist back his head
An he laugh, so we know dat dere's no sense to be scared.

And he never talk stories, he was all hana-hana[63]
An he fill up da ekes[64] full wit toys and bannanas.

Den he put his fat finger on top of his maka
But since never had smoke-stack he went jump out da puka.[65]

He jump in da canoe, "Hoe, hoe!" he stay cry
Da menehunes[66] start to row. .. dey take off in da sky.

And dey chanted dis mele,[67] heard all over Hawaii
"Mele Kalikimaka and to all Aloha Ahi-Ahi!"[68]

---

[62] eyes
[63] work
[64] bags
[65] door
[66] little men, Hawaii's elves
[67] song
[68] "Merry Christmas to all, and to all a Good Night!"

Keaka an da Lilikoi[69] Vine

Keaka lived Kapaa town on fah away Kauai
     My Tutu-man[70] tole me dis tail an Tutu-man no lie.
Keaka was won pooah, pooah boy but hiz branes was smaht an fine
     So I goin tell you now bout him an da lilikoi vine.

Da mama send dis keed to town for sell some poi an honey
     Da reezon waz dat dey is broke and badlee kneeds da money.
But Keaka meet one kahuna[71] man, an dey dickah den dey trade
     Da honey an poi for sum lilikoi seeds an da deel is klose an made.

How da spocks went fly wen da keed he reech home
     Mama lantern hiz eye an raze lumps on hiz dome.
But Keaka got kool hed an when kum da nite
     He planting da seeds by da kerasene lite.

An wen een da morneen heez godden, he look
     Da lilikoi growed to da hevvens… stay hook.
So he ware on hiz malo,[72] den he say wun kwick prayah
     Wiki-wiki[73] he klime for see what get up deah.

Wen he reech da top, he stay fine one big land
     Beeg mountain an tree an beeg palass so grand.
An hees eye stay pop out but hiz body hang loose

---

[69] passion fruit
[70] grandfather
[71] priest
[72] loin cloth
[73] quickly

Den he heah one "honk-honk" and he no gat wun goose.

So he sneek een da palass, he kroll on da floah
    He spy thru the keyhole eensigh of da door.
An dere on da chare wit da goose on his nee
    One big monstah giant iz singing wit glee.

Get wun reel sharp geetar playin all by eetself
    Wit sum julerys an diemons all ovah da shelf.
An az he stay peekin, Keaka behole
    Dat akamai[74] ne'ne[75] lay egg sollid gole.

An da giant stay singhing an laffin "hee-hee"
    "I'm da richess ole giant een all historeee."
"I get joolries an gooses an majick geetar!"
    An he pounding his poi an he laffin, "Har-har!"

Den he suck up da oke,[76] een wun hour heez sleepin
    an Keaka he kum een da rume heez a creepin.
He skoop up da jools an da geetah to boot
    To da lilikoi vine he stay run fass afoot.

As he klime down da vine he stay peek lilikois
    Wen he breeng bak dis lute his folks jumpeen wit joys.
But Keaka's not pau cause he no can foahget
    Da pooah ne'ne goose cuz he likeum foah pet.

So up he stay klime to dat lann in da skys
    Sneeks eensigh da joint like one fox on da slys.
Whea da giant stay sleepin he kapchure da goose
    An da goose stay supprize so wit "honks" he let loos.

---

[74] smart
[75] Hawaiian goose
[76] booze

Keaka stay skared, all his bakin is shakin
    An da giant jump up an da skie is a quakin.
Heez stomppin his feets all ovah da grownd
Dats why londin breedge been was staht fai-lin' down.

"FEE, FI, FO, FUM, AN ALOHA O'E!
    I smell wun onolishus[77] kanaka[78] boy."
"Alive or dead I'm going leeping wit joy
    Cause I'm grind heem all up for meex insigh my poi."

Den he leeft up da punee![79] Keaka went yell!
    Den he split out da puka[80] an running like hell,
Wit da momona[81] fat goose stuck eensigh of his blouse
    He klime down da vine like wun fass mickey mouse.

Da giant he yell til youah eah he kum soah
    "Breeng back my ole goose!" he stay skreem wit a roah.
Den da lilikoi vine he stay staht to klime down
    All da natives stay shakin in Kapaa Town.

Dat Keaka eez sharp, yes, heez rite on da stick
    He grab up wun cane-nife an chops wit a kwick.
Chop choppin he chop off da lilikoi trunk
    An da giant, he fall wit one urtquake KA TUNK!

He mak'e[82] die dead, nere Kapaa by dah sea
    An hiz boddee still stay dere for all us to see.
So, If you no beeleev, go Kapaa take a look
    At da ole sleeping giant, you'll reeley get shook.

---

[77] delicious
[78] human
[79] couch
[80] door
[81] fat
[82] dead

An Keaka was gude like one ole robbing hood
    Nobody went pooah in dat hole naborhood.
Every week he trow luau[83] wit hulas an laffter
    An he happily live from da then to da ever and after.

---

[83] feast

Da Tree Leedle Peegs

Een da moundtins up manoa side
Dis ole man got sum peegs
But tree of dem kud tock an seeng
As peegs, dey wuz beeg weegs!

Dey play an danse an surf all day
They's happee as kud bea
Til dat pilau[84] woluff kame o'deah
An make doze peegies flea.

Deze peegs wuz orfans now, you know
Kuz da peegs went gradjuashun
An da nice ole man went raze dem up
Went move to Maui nayshun.

So dey get no moah howse for go
An hide for dere protekshun
Dere force for formalate one plan
About dere life's projeckshun.

Da furstest peeg like dance da jeegs
An hula up all day
Wit beeg tin kups okolehao[85]
For chase hiz feahs away.

Big soah heez hade wen he wake up
But still he danse da jeegs
Waz hod time wurk an danse same time
So he bild heez howse of tweegs.

Da seckon peeg was playbuoy tipe

---

[84] stinky, smelly
[85] liquor distilled in Hawaii

All time puff pakalolo[86]
For strengt he bilt wit wooden boards
Bekos heez hapa-lolo.[87]

Da terdest peeg was plenny smaht
He make hiz howse wit rocks
Konkrete dem een wit iron bars
An xtra strong-kine lox.

(time marches on)

Da woluff went kum to da firss peeg howse
He nox up on da doah
An den he talk dis story
Dat wuz nevvah hurd befoah.

(Woluff) "Leedle peegie puaa,[88] I like foah kum een!"
(Peegy) "No! Not by da hairs on my cheeny cheen chin!"
(Woluff) "Den I'll huffah an puffah an bloe youah howse down!"

An sune he puff, da howse went ka pow!
He throwed da peeg een da imu,[89] an had wun luaua.

Aftah wun weak, da woluff hungahs foah fude
Hiz opu stay stahtin to grind
He saw pokchops an cha siu an black bean rost pok
An what iz mor onolishus,[90] da rind.

Dat seckon peeg stay smelling rats
Runz home, lox up da doah

---

[86] crazy weed [lit.], marijuana
[87] half-crazy
[88] pig
[89] underground oven
[90] tasty, good, delicious

An heez so skared, heez hidin dea
Heez bacon on da floah.

(Woluff) "Ho-hoo leedle peeg, I'll be pleezd to kum in!"
 (Peegy) "No, not by the hare on my cheeny cheen chin!"
(Woluff) "Den I'll whiff an I'll poof an I'll blow youah howse down!
Da howse went kollaps, an peeg wuz roasted brown.

Now, da terd leedle peeg, wow! Dis buggah wuz smaht
He boil puna-wai[91] een wun u'-ka-beeg pot
Stuck it dere een da fiah plase, rite undah da hole
Foah dat woluff heez now reddy, so he go take a stroll.

Wen da woluff he sparkin da porkah a' strollin
He sheeft geahs to kompoun an full speed kums a'rollin
But da terd leedle peeg, he went jump on heez byke
Leff da woluff standin steel, even dough he no like.

Wen he reech hiz rock hale, peegy kwick lox da doah
Puts paakai[92] an spyce, by da pot on da floah
Den he chop sum bodadoes an sellery two
An wit seex pounds fresh poi gonna make woluff stu!

Soon dat woluff, he went kum to da terd peegy's howse
Heez foamin frum hiz jawz
He can awreddy tase dat bobbequ pok
Stay melting een heez paws.

(Woluff) "Hoo-hoo porky peeg, I like for kum een!"
 (Peeg) "No, not by da hares on my cheeney chin cheen!"
So da woluff puff an he blow, but da howse no fall down
An da woluff stay poop-out frum huffin aroun.

---

[91] spring water
[92] salt

Da woluff still stay stahv so he tink of wun hay he
Kan kaptcher da peeg foah make pokchop an grayvee
So he klime up da rufe top for get hun gude looka
Hiz shop eye, it went spock up da fiyah plase puka.[93]

Da woluff hed-furst went...neva look befoah leep
Een da pot he went land... surve heem rite, da dum kreep,
So da terd leedle peegy he went covah da pot
Til da woolf turn to stu meat, so tendah an hot!!!

Den peegie trowed pahty foah all of da town
For myles dey stay kum frum da kuntree surround
Dey eet til deah mout broke an dey inu-up[94] too
Yeah, dey all sellebrate kuz dat woluff's een da stew!

An dat terd leedle peeg a talkin majishun
He stay make one beeg speech, he like be politikshun
So for kongress he runned frum ole Hawaii-nei
An da peeg elexted! Pig-pig-pig-pig hooorae!!

Onnerable peegie da terd, he shuah wuz sum smaht
He pass one beeg lawz wit Hawaii at heart
All da woluffs waz bannd frum fare Hawaii-nei
An dat law steel affeck us frum den 'til today!

No fore legged woluffs stay allow een our aina
Da too legged kine? No can help.. .Dey are minah.
Dey are luvahs, not fiters! Wit dere teets dey no eat u
Yeah, dere wepons are wurds. .. maybe fun for defeet u.

Leedle peegie retire, says, "My job is pau[95] now!"
Fell een luv an he marry one real porky sow,
Dey had keeds by da dozens, fine pile-a-oinkers

---

[93] chimney
[94] drink up
[95] finished

But dats peegie style an dey nevah went boinkers!!

Yeah, da terd leedle peeg
Wuz one bone-a-fyde hero
Da pilau[96] beeg bad woluff
Ended up battin zero.

Yess, I'm tellin da trute
An eef u tink I lie
Find wun woluff (4-legged) in Hawaii
U weel look till u die!!!

---
[96] stinky

Da Tree Bares

Da Kahuna say in da olden day
Hawaii get tree bares
Dey live eenside da mountain place
Wit house, bowls, bed, and chairs.

One day one tourist haole[97] broad
Ner name was Goldie Laka[98]
Went walk inside da forest place
An all twist up her maka[99].

"Auwe,"[100] she cry, "Auwe, auwe!"
"I tink I loose my way!"
An den she spark da hale[101]
Where dose tree bares always stay.

Dis haole babe, she go eensigh
She taste da tree poi[102] bowl
Da papa's poi was too damn hot
Da mama's too damn cole.

Da keiki's[103] poi was jussa rite
She eat one treeple share,
When pau[104] da poi she went relax
And she bust da small bare chair.

---

[97] caucasian
[98] Goldie Locks
[99] eyes, eyesight
[100] alas, oh dear
[101] house
[102] edible paste from the taro root
[103] child's
[104] finished

Now dis wahine,[105] Hawaiian style,
Her opu[106] full wit poi
She find tree bed, one hard, one soft
On da terde she hia-moee.[107]

Da bares kum home for wash dere clodes
One muumuu,[108] diapah, and malo[109]
But when dey look da poi stay eat
Dey never give mahalo.[110]

An when dey look da bust up chair
more hi, da sparks went flew
Da dirty buggah going catch hell
When da bares, dem find out who.
Da keiki bare, he give some screems
"O'hea, o'hea, o'hea!"
And Goldie Laka she wake up
And she try for dissapeah.

She scream her lung and den she leep
From punee[111] onto da floor
And wit da swift she crawl and run
Outsigh da kitchun doah.

But papa bare he wild like hell
An he trow hiss butt hi geah
An soon he stay catching dat dolly up
For her skeen I stay sadly feah.

---

[105] woman
[106] stomach
[107] fell asleep
[108] woman's dress
[109] loin cloth
[110] thank you
[111] couch

"Help! Help!" she cry, "I no like die!"
Cries split da air both near and far,
An lucky ting John Wayne went heah
Da cries from Kahala Hilton bar.

He grab his gun, jump on hiz hoss
Up da mountain place he flew
Heez trusty 6-gun shoot 10 times
As da Boy Scout bugle blew.

Da papa bare, now really bare
As da bullet went shoot off his malo
"Shame on you, dere, bare bare," she cried
An da bare took off... he was yullow.

So brave John Wayne rescue Goldie Laka
Dis sweet young tourist lady
I would tell you some more but the censors say no!
As da rest of da storie is shady.

Aloha!

Da Kolohe Mo'o of da Wailuka Rivah
(The Mischievous Lizard of the Wailuka River)

Maui stay on Maui iland
Hiz mumma she stay Hilo
She makin kapa[112] all day long
An kalabashes[113] of milo.[114]

Her howse wuz cave behind da falz
Of da reevah Kalled Wailuku
An her ladee frenz dey stay wit hur
Iz wun sweenging bunch of tutus.[115]

Butt she had wun lizzid anamee
Wun giunt.. . kuna mo'o
Who allatime trowing rox at hur
Kaus he like for broke her po'o.[116]

One nyte heez trowing pohakus[117]
An az uzuwal dey mees
An Hina[118] stahts een laffin
Kuna mo'o,[119] heez all kissed!!

So he grine heez jaws wit angree

---

[112] tapa, a cloth made from tree bark
[113] bowls
[114] a type of wood found in Hawaii
[115] grandmothers
[116] head
[117] rocks, stones
[118] Maui's mother
[119] supernatural fresh water lizard

Pili[120] full speeds down da pali[121]
He rolls down wun beeeg pohaku[122]
For dam up da reevah walley.[123]

An da Hina's bunch stay sleep up
Nevah heah dat mo'o klown
But da mo'o now stay happee
Koz wen rivah rize, dey drown.

For Hina kame da shi-shi time
An she open up her aye,
She stay spocked da rivah rizin
An she seeng out to da sky.

"Kum, Maui, kum wit youah mitie klub
Kum kweek in youah sweef kanoe
Eeef you no reech heah sune enuff
Youah moma, she is thru!!"

An Maui hurd hur een hiz dreem
Knowed moma wuz get trubbles
He trowed heez laigs in da nacheral gear
He wuz kumming on da dubble.

He throwd hiz klub een hiz fass kanu
He went paddal perpacheral motion
More faster den two hundred hoss
He kross pacific's ocean.

Wen he reech wailuku reever moutt
He spock up, "da reevahs dry"
Den he knowed da reevah all damn up

---

[120] close to
[121] cliff
[122] stone
[123] valley

Knowed dat mo'o gott for die.

Wen he looked da stone went skrew tings up
Dere wuz no time den for moov um
Wit heez beeg war klub he pound da banks
An aroun da rox he gruved um.

So dah rivah runned, all da dainjah pau[124]
Butt for now, wheas kuna mo'o?
But dat lizzahd skared an hidin
In one unnerwatah grotto.

Sune Maui smelled da mo'o's steenk
Butt da pool too deep for reechum
So he got ideaz for smoke him owt
Dat mo'o, gotta teechum.

Maui run wit da sweeft, volcanoside
An he borrow from Aunty Pele
Hot lava for trow eenside da pool
So dat mo'o's gotta hele.

Da lava flowed an da potts wuz boil
Kuna mo'o koodn't stan eet
Koz hiz hans an laig an tale stay burn
He wuz a mos' deejekted bandit!
So da mo'o runned 'til he reech da falz
He stay caught so he must fur battle
Butt Maui's klub, klub dat mo'o's hed
An hiz branze dey all stay rattle!!

Maui's klub, klub-klub again
Rapp da mo'o een da hade
Ho' olei[125] da mo'o ower dah falz

---

[124] over, finished
[125] threw

He stay make', died, he's dead!!

An da mo'o's bodee still stay dere
For all us guize go look
An da pukas[126] wear da lava flowed
Still bubbling een da brook.

Yess, Maui he eez quite a guy
He luvs for play da jokeums
Butt for da krooks, when he's huhu[127]
Dere okoles,[128] he juss brokeums!!!

---

[126] holes
[127] angry
[128] rear end, buttocks

Simple Simon's Pieman

Lolo[129] Kaimana met da mea'ono pua'a[130] man-a
Going E.K Fernandez kine fair.
Said Lolo Kaimana to da mea'ono pua'a man-a
I stay starving for taste of you ware.

Da mea'ono pua'a man-a, he tell Lolo Kaimana
"Show first me your keni-ken."[131]
Said Lolo Kaimana to da mea'ono pua'a man-a
"Ho bruddah! I no stay get any."

Peter Piper's Peppers, da Kine Pidgin

Pika paika pika packa pikal papah
A paka pikal papah pika paika peek
If pika paika pika paka pikal papah
Wheada paka pi kal papah pika paika peek?

---

[129] stupid (slang)
[130] tasty bread with pork
[131] ten cents

Akeke Ella
(Cinderella)

Een Honolulu's kuahiwes[132]
Dere wuz wun nyce kine hale[133]
Da vu kood sea da see beech
An da reewa in da walley.
But dis howse stay nevah hapee
Cos o'deah wuz liv 4 sistahs
An da oldah 3 mayk da yung wun wurk
Till her han stay fool wit bleestahs.

Akeke Ella iz hur name
An dey treet hur like won slave
All day shee hana skrub da plase
An shee try for ack so brave
Koz hur pelapela[134] sistahs
Of hur buetee, dey stay jellus
So dey buss hur up an slapp hur down
My Tutu Man[135] went tell us.

Tita[136] 1 was fatso
    As momona[137] az kan bea
An Tita 2 wuz skeeny,
    Da Hawaiians say wi-wi[138]
An Tita 3 wuz bend an tweest
    An her teets wuz nihomole[139]
But Ella wuz wun klassy lass

---

[132] mountains, high hills
[133] house
[134] nasty
[135] grandfather
[136] sister (slang)
[137] fat
[138] thin, skinny
[139] her teeth were missing

Frum hed to hur okole.[140]

Hark! Hark! One day da pupuhi[141]
    Went blass da trummpet soun
Da peeples kame a gaddering
    Frum all da kuntree round.
Da alii[142] cheef goin trow luau
    Wit okolehao[143] an swipe[144]
Bekoz da sun made 21
    For get married, gettin ripe.

Da Titas tree gets da lio[145] whip
Make Ella pound da kapa[146]
So dey kan make nice kine muumuus[147]
An holokus[148] of tapa
An da Titas Tree, dey all shiek up
Nu klodes frum hair to toe
An Ella say, "I like go, too."
But da Titas Tree say "no!"

Da time iz kum, da mahina[149] shine
Da lama[150] lite da ala[151]

---

[140] buttocks, rear end
[141] trumpet shell
[142] chief, chieftess, king, queen
[143] liquor made from ti root
[144] raw fruit liquor
[145] horse
[146] tapa
[147] woman's dress
[148] dress with a train
[149] moon
[150] torch
[151] way

Get hapa[152] duzzen imus[153]
Wit uala,[154] peegs an kala[155]
An sowwa poi, he luau
An beeg kalua ulu[156]
Dis wuz da beegess luau
Evah seed in Honolulu.

Da Titas Tree, dey potty go,
Tey teenk dey luke so klassy
Wit all kine flowah een dere hare
An leis all oer dere chassis
An all da luvahly ladeez
Of Oahu kame a' prancing
Dey all like ketch da hannsum prinz
Wit ami hula dantsing.

Akeke Ella stay stuk home
Hur maka[157] full wit teers
Dere's nutting on dis eartly eart
Kan full hur hot wit cheers.
"Eh, pehea oe?"[158] wen feel da air
Wen Ella spock hur eye
An deah wuz Tutu Pele[159]
Kummin down frum up da sky.

"I am youah fairee Tutu Ma," Pele wen tell to Ella
"how kum you no wear on nyce klodes,
Try skoop dat young printz fellah?"

---

[152] half
[153] underground oven
[154] sweet potato
[155] unicorn fish
[156] steamed breadfruit
[157] eyes
[158] "How are you?"
[159] volcano goddess

"Auwe, auwe[160], I no moah lei
An no moah nyce sarong
An no moah pa' a kama' a[161]
For wock da rode along."

"Kulilkuli,[162] sealy chile,"
Da Tutu Ma went tell
"Go find me 4 iole nui[163]
An 2 small kine as well.
Frum da godden breen beeg ipu[164]
An sum large size spidah web
An garandtee dis potty,
You goin bee won 1st klass deb!"

So da prinz talk matrimonial
Wile da pahu[165] beat won dozzen
Den Ella, she remembah
Trows her tale in geah, sheez buzzin
Fool speeed ahade hur feets stay fly
Til wun small size branch wen treep hurt
"Uwe, uwe!" Ella kry,
"I looze my hula slippah!!"

An she find da kaa-lio[166]
Stay turn back to won amole[167]
An da hosses an deah drivahs
Turn back to small iole[168]

---

[160] grieve, groan, bewail
[161] pair of shoes
[162] be quiet, shut up
[163] rats
[164] gourd
[165] drum
[166] horse-drawn coach
[167] gourd, bottle
[168] rats

An da spidah webb dat spun hur drass
Wuz krummee bunch of raggs
An pooah Akeke Ella
Shee wuz dress juss like a hags.

Wen da Titas Tree kum back da hale[169]
All dey kan doo is wondah
"Who wuz da babe dat skupe da prints
Who kozzed heez hade to dundah?"
Dey arr nastee meen to Ella
Make hur all skrubb up da floah
An den dey leek hur wit da weep
An make hur skrub summoaha.

Aftah bout wun week da cheef's pu-puhi[170]
Blass out da trumpeet kall
An all da land's wahines[171]
Kum an gadder een da mall
Dey stay look see a peelow
Wut stay make from soff lauhala[172]
An onntop stay gat one sleepah
No kan feet da avridge fullah.

Da wahines all stay try ware on
Dees luvvaly, tynee shooo
Deah feets 2 beeg, 2 long, 2 shoart
Dere's nuttin dey kan doo.
For make eet feet, dey evan tri
For kut off kupple tow
But da beeg maka'i[173] say, "Nix on dat!
No feah! Da ansser's no!"

---

[169] house
[170] trumpet shell
[171] women
[172] pandamus leaves
[173] policeman

An doze Titas Tree, pooah Ella
No stay lend hur kum outsigh
Dey lox hur een da keetchen
Poundin kalo[174] 'til shee kry
Butt her talkin kolo[175] mynah burd
Flyd down an sqweel da beens
Den da alii's beeg maka'i[176]
Tared apaht dose keetchen skreenz.

Akeke Ella wuz seetin dere
Poundeen pa'i' ai[177]
Da kalo splashd up on hur fase
Frum neck to beddrume aye
Da beeg maka'i[178] geev komman,
"Kumm owt foah tri da shoo
An eef kan fitt youah luau feet
Da printz like peetch da woo."

Akeke Ella kame outsigh
She wuz wipin off da tears
An den she sawed won sumting dat
Wen feel her hot wit cheers.
For dere on top wun peelow
She went spock won fantzee shooo
Won tini small Adidas
An da colorz spocklin blue.

Hur kries of joys went spleet da air
"My shoo, my shoo," she cryd
"I loozed um at da printses' ball

---

[174] tapa
[175] a name, call
[176] chief, policeman
[177] hard, pounded taro before adding water
[178] policeman

Ass wy I'm seek eensighd."
An she sleeped eet on, won purfeck feet
An da krowd weet happies cryd
Koz pooah Akeke Ella
Gonna be da preences bride.

An da beeg pupuhi[179] blass an blass
Da preence kame run o' dere
He propozishun Ella
For be hiz mayden fare.
An Ella took won luke an swooon
Bekoz she wuz hauoli.[180]
An all da peeples danse and cheer
Bekauz dey all stay 'oli.[181]

An Ella's ferry Tutu Ma[182]
Wen speen sum wheelah deelahs.
She errupshunned up da boilahs
Een gude ole Kaimana Mila.[183]
An she rumble up sum urt qwakes
Wit a wicked hula sweeng,
An it stahted church bells ringing
Wit a swing a ding dong ding.

Akeke Ella, she say "Yes!
I'm ono[184] deeah, for u."
So kahuna nui[185] preyd out one preyah
For make wun out of 2.
An so, da preentz an Ella,

---
[179] trumpet shell
[180] happy
[181] happy
[182] grandmother
[183] Diamond Head
[184] savor, crave
[185] high priest

Dey went tell da beeg "I DO"
An wun tinee, preety sleepah
Eez wut maked it all kum troo!!

Yes, da luv smyles krossd dere fases
Eet stay stretch from eah to eah
An I'm tole da hunny-mooon wen lass
For ovah feefty ears,
An Oahu nei[186] stay prospah
Undah happie, luvvin leedahs
Kos Tutu Pele went inwent
Doze sleepahs kalld Adidas!!!

Pau[187] now.

---

[186] Oahu here
[187] finished

Kauai, scene from Kalalau Trail

www.ingramcontent.com/pod-product-compliance
Lightning Source LLC
Chambersburg PA
CBHW051256110526
44589CB00025B/2847